An Illustrated History of the
Atlantic Coast Express

An Illustrated History of the

Atlantic
Coast Express

John Scott Morgan

OPC

An imprint of
Ian Allan Publishing

In memory of John Ernest Geach, 1938-2007.
A good friend and LSWR / Southern enthusiast who for 30 years
was Secretary of the Model Railway Club, London.

Half title: **Bulleid Light Pacific No 34062** *quadron* **at Padstow in the summer of 1958.** *Patrick Kingston*

Title page: **'Merchant Navy' No 35003** *Royal Ma* **on the up 'ACE' storms up Honiton Bank on the approach to Honiton Tunnel on 3 September 1949. The carriage formation on this train is noteworthy, with two restaurant vehicles heading a mixture of Maunsell and Bulleid stock.** *M. Whitehouse collection*

Front cover: **East of Exeter Bulleid's 'Merchant Navy' Pacifics were the staple motive power for the 'Atlantic Coast Express' in the postwar era. Bound for Waterloo, No 35026** *Lamport & Holt Line* **passes Seaton Junction on 11 July 1959.** *R. C. Riley*

Back cover: **Weight restrictions in north Devon and Cornwall dictated the use of Bulleid's Light Pacifics west of Exeter. On 6 July 1961 'West Country' No 34011** *Tavistock* **passes Cowley Bridge Junction with the Padstow and Bude portion of the up 'Atlantic Coast Express'.** *R. C. Riley*

Above: **Class N15 'King Arthur' No 776** *Sir Galagars* **at speed with a down West of England express at Hersham on 16 June 1938. The carriage formation is of interest, with early-pattern bogie panel stock and a mix of early-pattern LSWR and Maunsell steel-bodied stock.** *Ian Allan Library*

Right: **'Merchant Navy' No 35013** *Blue Funnel* **leaves Salisbury with an up 'ACE' on 22 August 1948. Just months after nationalisation, the locomotive has already been fitted with a smokebox numberplate. Note the original style of train headboard.** *The Rev C. Cawston / R. K. Blencowe collection*

First published 2010

ISBN 978 0 86093 634 3

All rights reserved. No part of this book may be reproduced or transmitted in any form or by any means, electronic or mechanical, including photocopying, recording, scanning or by any information storage and retrieval system, on the internet or elsewhere, without permission from the Publisher in writing.

© Ian Allan Publishing Ltd 2010

Published by Ian Allan Publishing

An imprint of Ian Allan Publishing Ltd, Hersham, Surrey KT12 4RG.
Printed in England by Ian Allan Printing Ltd, Hersham, Surrey KT12 4RG.

Distributed in Canada and the United States of America by BookMasters Distribution Services.

Code: 1005/B1

Visit the Ian Allan Publishing website at www.ianallanpublishing.com

Contents

Foreword

The train that came to be known as the 'Atlantic Coast Express' can trace its origins to the golden age of railways in the 1890s and was romanticised in the 1920s by the newly formed Southern Railway as taking the scenic route to the West Country. Between the wars John Betjeman's family always travelled Southern when taking their holidays in the West Country, and his autobiographical poem 'Summoned by Bells' immortalises their journey from Waterloo to 'far Trebetherick', near Padstow on the North Cornwall coast. Now John Scott-Morgan has given us the definitive book on this famous train, providing not only a highly readable account of its history and route but also 250 largely unpublished photographs which gloriously enrich his theme.

The 'ACE' was famed for its complexity, leaving Waterloo with up to 13 coaches and arriving at Padstow with just one, having dropped at least five portions *en route*. As well as relating the history of the train — explaining how it was named by a guard, whose suggestion was the winning entry in a Southern Railway competition — John describes the development of the lines over which it ran. In so doing he recalls the destructive rivalry that flared up at times between the Great Western and the LSWR/SR as they squabbled over the long-distance market to Exeter and Plymouth — something he links with the eventual demise of the 'ACE' just after the line from Salisbury to Exeter was transferred

to the Western Region. Twelve years later I was Operations Manager on the South Western Division, and I well remember the bitter disappointment that was still felt by South Western staff over the downgrading of their flagship main line.

Although concerned principally with the 'ACE' John does not overlook its sister train, including a section on the the 'Devon Belle', which was one of the first Pullman services to be restored after World War 2 and became an icon of postwar recovery. This is followed by a detailed, copiously illustrated description of the route of the 'ACE' all the way from Waterloo to the furthest extremities of Southern territory in north Devon and Cornwall. And, as a bonus, we get first-hand accounts from those who remember using the train in their earliest days.

All in all it is a fascinating story, culminating in the withdrawal of the 'ACE' in September 1964 and the singling, as part of a short-sighted economy drive, of much of its route. It is therefore especially fitting that the book should be published at the very time that Network Rail is re-doubling part of the South Western main line between Salisbury and Exeter. Who knows … we may one day see the return of a flagship service on the route, albeit probably not one that splits into five portions!

Chris Green
Berkhamsted, January 2010

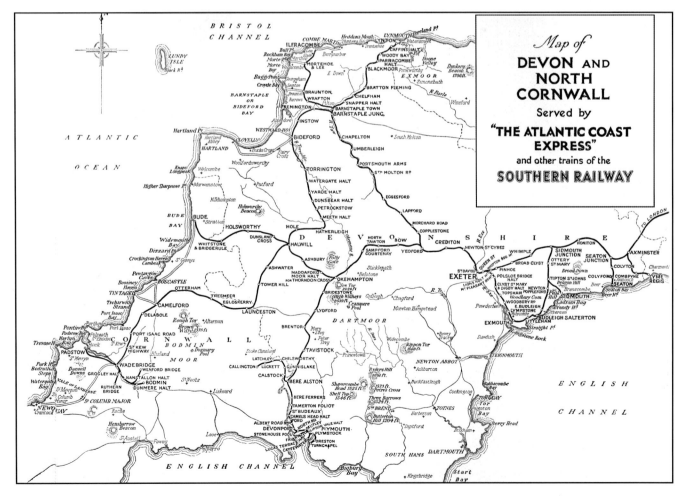

Map of DEVON AND NORTH CORNWALL Served by "THE ATLANTIC COAST EXPRESS" and other trains of the SOUTHERN RAILWAY

Introduction

In the summer of 1973, along with my friend John Geach, I made a journey from Paddington to Totnes. After visiting the Dart Valley Railway (then at an early stage of development) we decided to go on to look at the former London & South Western Railway terminus at Plymouth Friary. After closure to passengers in September 1958 the station had been used by the Western Region as a goods and parcels depot, and in 1973 the infrastructure was still in quite good condition, having only recently been vacated. The trackwork was still recognisably the LSWR/Southern layout, and the platforms and buildings — still in faded Southern Region green-and-cream — stood forlorn but intact; all that was missing was the signs and signals, which had by then been removed for scrap or reuse. The station's faded charm held a peculiar fascination, and, more than anything else, it was this visit that sparked my interest in the Southern's operations in the West Country, known (even before the closures of the 1950s and '60s) as the 'Withered Arm'.

Perhaps on account of the places it served, the 'Atlantic Coast Express' will always have a particular appeal. Although the name did not appear until 1926, the origins of the 'ACE' date back to the dawn of rail's golden age, which began in the late 19th century and continued until the outbreak of World War 2. This was an era when most people travelled long distances by train and were used to a high level of service from the companies that operated Britain's railway network. The 'ACE' was well up to the task, providing its passengers with a first-class service with premier facilities including a full dining car with a fine selection of dishes on the menu. It was, moreover, quite unlike any other named train of its time, in that it served so many locations using carriage stock that left London's Waterloo station as a single formation.

For almost four decades the 'ACE' ranked alongside the other famous Southern expresses — the 'Brighton Belle', 'Bournemouth Belle' and 'Golden Arrow' — and a gleaming 'King Arthur' (or, in postwar years, a rebuilt Bulleid Pacific) pounding up Honiton Bank at the head of a dozen or more bogie corridor carriages was a sight to behold. This book, in addition to chronicling the train's history, aims to convey something of the excitement and romance of travelling on the 'ACE'. I hope you enjoy the journey.

John Scott-Morgan
Woking
January 2010

Acknowledgements
In writing this book I have been aided by numerous individuals, and I should like to thank in particular Chris Green, Douglas Stuckey and John Power for their contributions to the text. I should like also to acknowledge the assistance provided by the National Archives at Kew, the Railway Club Library and the Model Railway Club Library, all of which have proved invaluable in verifying information. Photographers are credited individually at the end of each caption, and to all I extend my grateful thanks; in addition I should like to thank Christine Riley and Rodney Lissenden, for making available the collection of Christine's late husband, Dick. In the case of all photographs, every effort has been made to identify the copyright-holder, but anybody who has been omitted is invited to contact me via the publisher.

Bibliography
BR Pre-Grouping Atlas and Gazetteer (Ian Allan, 1958)
Transport of the 40s: Southern Locomotives (Ian Allan, 1968)
From the Footplate: Atlantic Coast Express, Stephen Austin (Ian Allan, 1989)
The London & South Western Railway Volumes 1 and 2, R. A. Williams (David & Charles, 1968 and 1973)
The LSWR in the 20th Century, J. N. Falkner and R. A. Williams (David & Charles, 988)
The History of the Southern Railway, M. Bonnavia (Unwin & Hyman, 1987)
The Okehampton Line, J. Nicholas and G. Reeve (Irwell Press, 2001)
The Ilfracombe Line, J. Nicholas (Irwell Press, 1998)
The Bude Branch, D. J. Rowe (Kingfisher, 1988)
Sir Herbert Walker's Southern Railway, C. F. Clapper (Ian Allan, 1973)
Locomotives at the Grouping (Southern), H. C. Casserley (Ian Allan, 1968)
Locomotives of the LSWR Volumes 1 and 2, D. L. Bradley (Railway Correspondence & Travel Society, 1965 and 1967)
Locomotives of the Southern Railway Volumes 1 and 2, D. L. Bradley (Railway Correspondence & Travel Society, 1976)
Portrait of the Atlantic Coast Express, Stephen Austin (Ian Allan 1997)

Construction and development of the route

The gradual construction of the London & South Western route to the far reaches of the West Country has much to do with the political and financial relationship between the LSWR and the Great Western Railway. The two companies eyed each other with considerable suspicion, the GWR and its associated companies — primarily the Bristol & Exeter Railway and the Cornwall Railway — being determined to keep out the LSWR at all costs, regarding Devon and Cornwall as their preserve.

The LSWR had had designs on the West Country since its earliest days. Having reached Basingstoke it commissioned a survey to plan a route to Bath via Newbury and Devizes and sought parliamentary powers necessary to construct the line, thereby causing an open dispute with the GWR, which regarded the area from Newbury to Bath and Bristol as its own domain — this despite the fact that the London & Southampton Railway (as the LSWR was known until 1839) had laid its first rails before the Great Western cut its first sod. This was merely the first of many such disputes between the two companies, and the bad feeling would continue until the late 19th century, when the LSWR finally constructed its last lines in Devon and Cornwall.

The proposed line to Bath never came to fruition, but Salisbury was reached in 1847 by means of a cross-country line from Bishopstoke, and the first section of what was to become the LSWR's West of England main line opened from Basingstoke to Salisbury via Andover on 1 May 1857. Further westerly extensions were built to Yeovil and Honiton, until Exeter was reached in July 1860. At this point, with the LSWR poised on the frontier of Great Western territory in Devon, and the South Devon Railway (the GWR's partner in the area) feeling uneasy with regard to its intentions, we must pause to consider developments further west.

The LSWR had made inroads into north Cornwall coast in 1847, when the company acquired the Bodmin & Wadebridge Railway (at that time more than 100 miles from the nearest LSWR station, at Dorchester) from under the nose of the Cornwall Railway, a broad-gauge line backed by the GWR. During the same period the LSWR also managed to gain control of the broad-gauge Exeter & Crediton Railway from another GWR associate, the Bristol & Exeter Railway, although in a strange twist of fate contractor Thomas Brassey, who had built the Exeter & Crediton and the North Devon Railway from Crediton to Barnstaple, leased the entire line to the Bristol & Exeter under an operating agreement, broadened to encompass the Bideford Extension Railway when the latter opened on 2 November 1855. The line was further extended to Ilfracombe in 1874.

Below: **Adams 'X6' 4-4-0 No 658 leaves Basingstoke *c*1907 with a London-bound express. The train is of interest, comprising a mixture of non-corridor bogie stock and vans immediately behind the locomotive. On the far right of the picture can be seen the overall roof of the Great Western station.** *SLS collection*

Right: **Tunnel Junction, Salisbury, *c*1910, with an up express emerging from the portal. The junction controlled the lines to Basingstoke and London (far right) and to Romsey and Southampton (left foreground).** *SLS collection*

Left: **The view west at Exeter Queen Street station (renamed Exeter Central after the Grouping). On the far right can be seen an Adams 'A12' ('Jubilee') 0-4-2, while on the centre road is an Adams 'T3' 4-4-0, and on the left a Drummond 'T9' 4-4-0. The over-complicated trackwork in the goods yard (far right) dates back to the period of railway history when the operating department dominated the Civil Engineering Department and could request impractical civil-engineering projects. Later the civil engineers gained the upper hand, and the practice ceased.** *Lens of Sutton Association*

Right: **Ilfracombe station c̶ ̶ ̶ ̶ ̶ving Drummond 'M7' 0-4-4T N̶ ̶ ̶ ̶ving the station with a four-car mi̶x̶ ̶ ̶ ̶of corridor and non-corrid̶o̶ ̶ ̶ock. The carriage sidings ar̶ ̶ ̶ ̶ ̶by a mixture of LSWR and̶ ̶ ̶ ̶riage stock, including a set̶ ̶ ̶ ̶ ̶nward 'toplight' bogie car̶ ̶ ̶ ̶re left) and a Dean gas-lit cle̶ ̶ ̶ ̶iage coupled to an LSWR non̶ ̶ ̶ ̶ogie vehicle (*far left*). On th̶ ̶ ̶ ̶be seen the single-road loc̶o̶ ̶ ̶shed and the turntable.** *Lens̶ ̶ ̶ton Associationa*

Over the next quarter-century the LSWR would construct a series of new lines across Devon and Cornwall, linking all the major towns and transport hubs to provide a network north of Exeter that was as comprehensive as that constructed in south-west Devon and Cornwall by the Great Western. Crucially, this also included Plymouth, with its important naval dockyard at Devonport. Only in 1888, however, was the isolated Bodmin & Wadebridge line finally connected the rest of the LSWR system.

By 1900 the LSWR had completed its routes to the emerging seaside resorts of Ilfracombe, in north Devon, and Bude and Padstow, on Cornwall's Atlantic coast. Following the opening of these latter, in the late 1890s, Okehampton became an important transport hub in north Devon, served by trains to London via Exeter and to Plymouth via Tavistock, as well as by those on the newly opened North Cornwall line. It also saw considerable cattle and farm-produce traffic, as well as military traffic from several camps in the area.

The final section of the route from London to the sea ran west from Okehampton across Meldon Viaduct to Meldon Junction, where the lines to the far West of England diverged; one ran south to Plymouth through Tavistock, the other continuing north-west to Halwill Junction, where there was another split, the more northerly line continuing to Bude, the other turning south towards Wadebridge and Padstow.

Just before the Grouping in 1923 the LSWR gained control of the hitherto independent Lynton & Barnstaple Railway, built in the 1890s to a gauge of 1ft 11½in, which brought access to Exmoor and the seaside resorts of Lynton and Lynmouth.

A late addition to the standard-gauge network was made in 1925 with the opening of the North Devon & Cornwall Junction

Railway, which connected Halwill Junction with Torrington. However, this was an independent concern, albeit run from an office at Waterloo and operated by the Southern as a light railway. This final piece in the railway jigsaw in the South West was engineered by Colonel Holman Fred Stephens, who was also involved in the upgrading and reconstruction of the Plymouth, Devonport & South Western Junction Railway from Bere Alston to Callington, which had become part of the LSWR in 1922.

Below: **Bude station in the summer of 1920, with Adams 'X6' 4-4-0 No 657 at the head of a local train for Okehampton and Exeter. The Bude and Padstow branches, both of which had opened in the late 1890s, were the final links in the LSWR's network of lines in the far South West.** *LCGB / Ken Nunn collection*

Right: **A photograph of Padstow station taken early in the 20th century, showing a train of non-corridor bogie passenger stock on the centre road and more passenger vehicles, probably from an excursion, in the background. The extensive goods and fish sheds can be seen centre right, and the newly built railway station and signalbox on the far left.** *SLS collection*

Below right: **Barnstaple Town station in the early 1930s. A Great Western train headed by a Churchward Mogul arrives from Taunton as a double-headed Lynton & Barnstaple Railway 2ft-gauge train, with Manning Wardle 2-6-2T No 760 *Exe* leading, awaits departure.** *Lens of Sutton Association*

Left: **'E1/R' 0-6-2T No 2124 crosses the Torrington Viaduct *c*1934 with a Halwill Junction–Torrington train. Note the remains of the Torrington & Marland Railway viaduct on the left.** *Lens of Sutton Association*

Centre left: **A view of Torrington station recorded during the winter of 1923/4 showing the station buildings, goods shed and track layout as they were before construction of the North Devon & Cornwall Junction Railway.** *Lens of Sutton Association*

Below: **Manning Wardle No 758 *Yeo* of the Lynton & Barnstaple Railway coasts downhill at Parracombe with a mixed train of bogie vans and carriage stock in the summer of 1934, only a year before this charming narrow-gauge line closed to all traffic.** *Author's collection*

Above right: **Beattie well tank No 3298 arrives at Wenford Bridge *c*1936 with a train of empty china-clay wagons. Of the three wagons at the front of the train the first is of Great Western origin, the second an ex-Great Eastern Railway van, and the third an eight-plank private-owner wagon with a coal delivery.** *Author's collection*

Right: **A photograph of Plymouth Friary *c*1925, early in the Southern Railway period, showing the track layout and signalbox. Note the two 'O2' 0-4-4T locomotives on station-pilot and local-train duty, as a Drummond 'T9' 4-4-0 (centre) prepares to depart with an up express.** *Lens of Sutton Association*

Origins of the 'ACE'

The LSWR was justifiably proud of its achievements in promoting and constructing, over a period of 65 years, a network of lines stretching from London to north Cornwall. However, by the late 19th century ideas as to how services on the South Western main line should be run were beginning to change from that of a basic train service to a railway with a variety of services to meet different traffic needs. Part of this reappraisal took the form of faster express services from Waterloo to Plymouth and the developing South West coastal resorts, which were becoming increasingly popular with our Victorian forebears, and with the opening in the late 1890s of the lines to Bude and Padstow came a clear need for a faster and more attractive service for those who wished to spend their holidays far from the smoke of London, on the golden sands of north Devon and Cornwall.

A century ago a journey to the far reaches of the LSWR's empire could take as long as four or five hours, often involving lengthy stops at principal stations for a change of locomotive or the detachment of carriage or van stock for a connecting service on a branch or secondary main line, and by the early years of the 20th century the LSWR had added dining cars to its important fast trains, greatly improving the quality of travel.

The GWR continued to feel aggrieved by the LSWR's presence west of Salisbury (specifically by the latter's acquisitions in the far South West, which it regarded as an intrusion on its territory), and it is difficult nowadays to imagine the intensity of the rivalry that existed a century ago over the Atlantic ocean mails and the fast Plymouth express services that were operated to serve this important traffic. However, relations between the two began to improve after the terrible accident at Salisbury on 1 July 1906,

Below: **A busy scene at the newly rebuilt Waterloo station *c*1920, with crowds of passengers boarding a 12-carriage West of England express. Beyond it can be seen a trio of Drummond locomotives, from right to left an 'L12' 4-4-0, an 'L11' 4-4-0 and an 'F13' 4-6-0 (partially obscured by the West of England stock), while on the left an Adams 'T1' 0-4-4T on station-pilot duty waits to shunt some vans as another 'T1' prepares to depart bunker-first with its train.**
Lens of Sutton Association

Above: **Representing the West of England expresses in the period immediately after World War 1, Urie 'N15' 4-6-0 No 739 speeds through Clapham Cutting *c*1921 with a train of mixed corridor and non-corridor bogie stock.** *SLS collection*

which cost the lives of 24 passengers and four staff and brought to an end the practice of racing boat trains between Plymouth and London. Indeed, following the Grouping in 1923 the Southern Railway and the GWR frequently co-operated over operating and traffic matters, a good example being the agreement permitting the latter's trains between Exeter and Plymouth to run via Okehampton, and the Southern's via the sea wall at Dawlish, so that, in the event of an emergency, crews from each company would be familiar with the other's route.

In some respects the Southern Railway got off to a bad start, having inherited a mixed bag of old and worn-out rolling stock, as well as some new modern equipment. Things took a while to change outwardly, and for the first year, apart from the odd locomotive or rake of coaches painted in the smart new livery of dark olive green, there was little change in each of the areas that made up the new company, the most noticeable change being tickets and publicity material at stations around the network.

In those early days the Southern came in for much criticism from the popular press, which often lambasted the company over operating issues — especially the organisation of its commuter trains and long-distance expresses, which in the opinion of contemporary news editors was sadly lacking.

Sir Herbert Walker, the Southern's General Manager, felt that a fresh approach was needed to improve the railway's image. He therefore recruited John Elliot, hitherto Assistant Editor of the *London Evening Standard*, to run the company's publicity department — an appointment that was to have a profound effect on the future of the Southern that was to continue into the BR era. Among other things, Elliot was responsible for the policy of naming the Southern's express locomotives (starting with the 'N15' 4-6-0s, which collectively became the 'King Arthur' class), prompting Chief Mechanical Engineer Richard Maunsell, to remark that, while he had no objection to the locomotives' being named, it would not make them run any faster! Most pertinent to our story, however, is the competition, held in 1925 at Elliot's behest, which determined that SR's principal train from London to the South West should be known henceforth as the 'Atlantic Coast Express'.

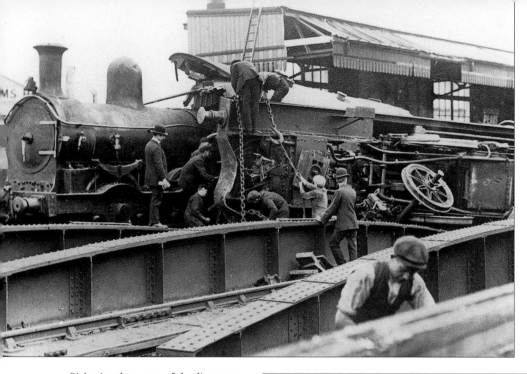

Left: A scene of carnage after the disaster at Salisbury on 1 July 1906, when the Plymouth–Waterloo boat train, running at excessive speed (estimated at 70mph) around the tight curve on the western approach, crashed into a milk train that was drawing into the station. Note the Beattie outside-frame 0-6-0 goods engine, No 0351, with Drummond 'L12' 4-4-0 No 421 lying on its side next to it, and the destruction of the station canopy.
R. K. Blencowe

Right: Another scene of the disaster at Salisbury on 1 July 1906, showing two of the steam cranes clearing the extensive wreckage of the boat train. One of the cranes is lifting the remains of a carriage underframe.
P. J. Fidczuk collection

Below: Train crashes were something of a spectator sport in Victorian and Edwardian times, hence the large number of local people avid for the gory details of the clear-up. The size of the crowd on the wall has to be seen to be believed. *P. J. Fidczuk collection*

The man who named the 'Atlantic Coast Express'

Dissatisfied with suggestions received for an appropriate name for its 11am departure from Waterloo to the West Country ('Devonian Express' etc) the Southern announced a competition for the title in the July 1925 issue of *Southern Railway Magazine*. The competition was won by Frederick Rowland, a guard at Waterloo, who was awarded three guineas — £3.15 in today's money but in the 1920s the equivalent of a week's wages — for 'Atlantic Coast Express'. Runners-up, from Nine Elms and Richmond, were each consoled with a paperweight in the form of a model 'King Arthur' 4-6-0.

Frederick Rowland was of Devonian origin. His father was a retired railwayman living at Topsham, but he also had family connections in North Devon. A year after winning his modest prize Frederick was transferred from Waterloo to Torrington — a move which, one surmises, had been at his own request.

Torrington was a hard-walking trudge from its station deep in the Torridge valley, but Rowland must have settled quickly, for the town's warm-hearted inhabitants elected him to the Town Council in 1927, when he headed the poll as a Ratepayers' Association candidate.

On Friday 9 September 1932 he was in charge of the 6.25am mixed train to Petrockstowe from Torrington, which stopped at Marland to pick up some loaded ball-clay wagons from a siding. There he had to alight, unlock the points, open a gate, and give the 'proceed' signal to the driver, John Slade (another Torrington man). Immediately after Slade received the go-ahead and moved forward, he looked back and saw Rowland lying on the cinder ballast between the rails; he had slipped on the greasy clay surface when releasing the wagon brakes, and a wagon had passed over him, breaking both his thighs. The fireman hurried to the clay works for help, but it was 25 minutes before men with a stretcher arrived on the scene. Rowland was taken first to the cottage hospital in Torrington, but his compound fractures and the necessary amputation of his left leg required better facilities, and he was moved to Bideford, where sadly he died of his injuries.

The *North Devon Journal* recorded that Rowland was a man held in high regard by all — even at the height of his agony, immediately after the accident, he had called out to his driver: "It was no fault of yours, Jack."

The title 'Atlantic Coast Express' did not disappear for good with the demise of the original train, and the enduring popularity of the name he chose — in recent years resurrected for trains to Newquay and used currently by FirstGroup for its X9 bus route from Exeter to Bude — serves as a fitting memorial to Frederick Rowland.

Above left: **'H15' 4-6-0 No 332**, pictured south of Woking in the 1930s, heads the 12.40pm to Plymouth. Note the interesting make-up of the train, with Maunsell Restriction 1 stock and ex-LSWR Surrey Warner panel stock in the consist. This locomotive was one of five Drummond 'F13s' rebuilt by Maunsell in 1924/5, the result being a considerable improvement. *Author's collection*

Left: Headed by 'King Arthur' 4-6-0 No 456 *Sir Galahad*, the 'ACE' runs through Milborne Port *c*1935. An interesting formation of 13 Maunsell steel-bodied carriages includes a dining-car set, which will be detached at Exeter and continue to Plymouth Friary. *Ian Allan Library*

Above: **'N15' 4-6-0 No 457** *Sir Bedivere* passing Yeovil Junction with the up 'ACE' in the summer of 1929. The train comprises a mix of ex-LSWR and early Maunsell corridor stock. *Author's collection*

Right: The up 'ACE' hauled by 'King Arthur' No 746 *Pendragon*, near Honiton Tunnel on 4 August 1928. The train comprises mainly wooden-panelled stock but also includes some Maunsell steel-bodied carriages and an ex-LSWR clerestory bogie dining car dating from the 1900s. *H. C. Casserley*

Left: 'H15' 4-6-0 No E332 speeds towards the darkness of Crewkerne Tunnel with an up West of England express on 2 August 1928. An unusual and remarkably brave photographic effort on the part of Mr Casserley— thankfully there wasn't a train coming the other way! *H. C. Casserley*

Below: Gleaming 'Scotch Arthur' No 792 *Sir Hervis de Revel* makes a fine sight as it awaits departure from Exeter Central in the summer of 1932 with an up London express consisting of equally beautifully painted and maintained Restriction 1 stock. *C. M. and J. M. Bentley collection*

Right: Adams 'X6' 4-4-0 No 665 at Barnstaple Junction station *c*1926 with a mixed rake of new Maunsell steel-bodied corridor carriages forming a train for Exeter. *SLS collection*

Below right: Plymouth Friary station in the summer of 1930: a train has just arrived from London, and a London-bound train, headed by a Maunsell Mogul, is about to depart from the other platform. Note 'T1' 0-4-4T No 16 on the centre road, an 'O2' 0-4-4T coupled to a pair of non-corridor carriages in the bay on the left, and the quantity of carriage stock in the sidings. *Lens of Sutton Association*

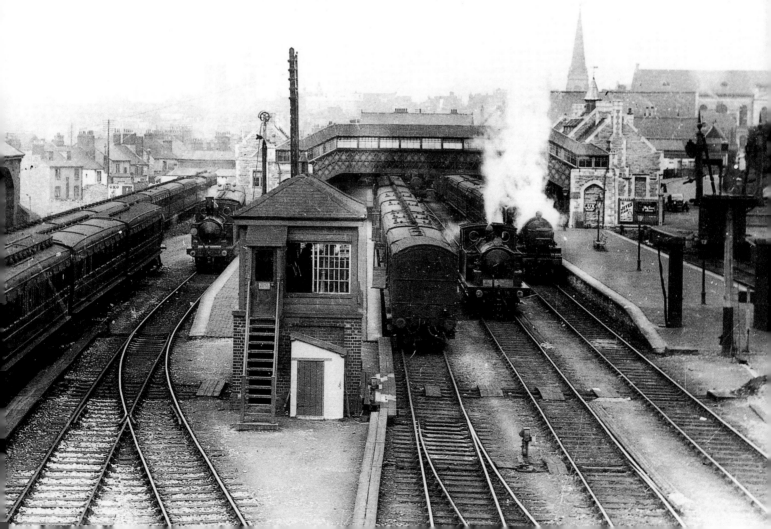

The postwar 'ACE'

Following the outbreak of war in September 1939 the 'Atlantic Coast Express' soon disappeared from the timetable and was replaced by the 10.50am train, which had additional stops and slower timings. This wartime train normally had from 10 to 13 carriages depending on whether the winter or the summer timetable was being operated. During this dark and uncertain period of Britain's history, the train carried mostly military personnel being located, relocated from one base to another, or going on leave; for Devon and Cornwall had large numbers of Army and Royal Air Force establishments in addition to the presence of the Royal Navy at Devonport dockyard near Plymouth.

The first tangible sign of postwar recovery came in the summer of 1947 with the introduction of the all-Pullman 'Devon Belle', which although not directly connected to the 'Atlantic Coast Express' covered much of its route.

The 'Atlantic Coast Express' itself reappeared in the timetable with effect from 6 October 1947. Departing Waterloo at 10.50am, it reached Salisbury (where through carriages for Seaton were detached) at 12.33pm and arrived at Exeter Central (where the restaurant car was detached) at 2.29pm. The Plymouth portion left Exeter Central at 2.46pm, calling at Exeter St Davids, North Tawton, Okehampton, Bridestowe, Lydford, Brentor, Tavistock, Devonport and Plymouth North Road, and terminated at Plymouth Friary at 4.55pm. The Ilfracombe/Torrington portion left Exeter Central at 2.34pm — before the detached Plymouth portion — and called at Exeter St Davids, Eggesford and, at 3.44pm, at Barnstaple Junction, where the Ilfracombe portion was detached. From here the Ilfracombe portion ran as an all-stations stopping service, reaching its destination at 4.36pm. The Torrington portion ran through from Barnstaple Junction, arriving at Torrington at 4.31pm. The 3.55pm all-stations connection from Okehampton to Bude and Padstow was not mentioned in the timetable.

In the up direction portions departed Padstow at 8.25am and Bude at 9.35am, combining at Halwill Junction and reaching Exeter Central at 12.05pm. Here, at 12.17pm, the train was joined by the Plymouth portion, which had left at 10am. In north Devon portions left Torrington and Ilfracombe at the same time (10.15am), combining at Barnstaple Junction for the journey south to Exeter Central, where, along with the restaurant car, they

Below: **The scene at Waterloo on 22 August 1945, with 'Merchant Navy' No 21C19** *French Line C.G.T.* **on a waiting train and a Portsmouth-bound '4-COR' electric multiple-unit on the far right. The train from which this photograph was taken probably had 14 or 15 carriages, being too long even for the generous platforms at Waterloo.** *H. C. Casserley*

Right: 'Merchant Navy' No 21C9 *Shaw Savill* **runs through Woking with a down West of England express in the summer of 1946. The station had been completely rebuilt in 1937, in conjunction with the electrification of the line to Alton.** *LCGB / Ken Nunn collection*

Below right: **An up West of England express, headed by 'N15X' 4-6-0 No 2332** *Stroudley* **in unrelieved wartime black, passes Brookwood on 5 October 1945. The train is a mixture of Maunsell steel-bodied stock and ex-LSWR Surrey Warner panelled stock.** *Author's collection*

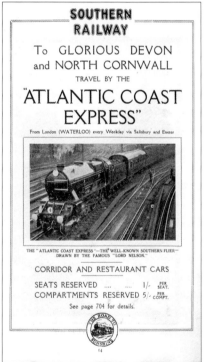

SOUTHERN RAILWAY

To GLORIOUS DEVON and NORTH CORNWALL

TRAVEL BY THE

"ATLANTIC COAST EXPRESS"

From London (WATERLOO) every Weekday via Salisbury and Exeter

THE "ATLANTIC COAST EXPRESS"—THE WELL-KNOWN SOUTHERN FLIER—DRAWN BY THE FAMOUS "LORD NELSON."

CORRIDOR AND RESTAURANT CARS

SEATS RESERVED .... 1/- PER SEAT.
COMPARTMENTS RESERVED 5/- PER COMPT.

See page 704 for details.

were added to the rest of the train. The complete formation then left Exeter at 12.40pm, calling at Sidmouth Junction, Axminster, Yeovil Junction, Sherborne, Templecombe and Salisbury, and reached Waterloo at 4.41pm.

Railway nationalisation in 1948 initially brought little change, but the early 1950s saw an upgrading of the line between Basingstoke and Exeter, and timings for the 'Atlantic Coast Express' were accelerated for the 1952 season, when the service became the first mile-a-minute express on the Southern Region. Leaving Waterloo at 11am, the train arrived at Salisbury in 83 minutes; Exeter Central was reached at 2.05pm, and, with improvements to the timetable, Ilfracombe by 4.10pm. The Torrington portion arrived at 4.04pm from Barnstaple Junction, and the Plymouth Friary portion arrived at 4.30pm from Exeter

Central. There were also considerable improvements in the up service. For example, the 9.50am departure from Plymouth Friary arrived at Waterloo at 3.40pm; this service included through carriages from Lyme Regis and Yeovil Town. With further timetable alteration during the mid-1950s, the western extremities of the Southern Region enjoyed probably the best express passenger service they had ever had.

Arrangements changed again with effect from 15 September 1958, when the Southern station at Plymouth Friary closed, services now terminating at North Road (the former Great Western station), now simply 'Plymouth'. During this period the connecting service to Bude and Padstow (generally comprising two or three carriages, depending on the time of year) appeared as an extra in the local timetable.

Above: **In filthy condition, 'Merchant Navy' No 21C9** *Shaw Savill* **lays down a long screen of sooty black smoke from poor fuel as it makes its way towards Basingstoke on the first leg of its journey to Exeter** *c*1946. **This photograph shows the locomotive in its initial all-black wartime livery; also the original style of air-smoothed casing (including the high-sided tender), which was designed to pass through carriage-washing plants.** *Author's collection*

Below: **'Merchant Navy' No 21C14** *Nederland Line* **makes a spirited start from Salisbury** *c*1947 **with an up West of England express made up of Maunsell Restriction 1 stock. The flat roof of the signalbox on the right had been designed in wartime as an emplacement for anti-aircraft guns.** *LCGB / Ken Nunn collection*

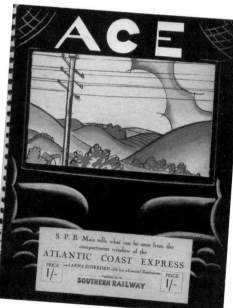

Above: **The Southern Railway published several books to accompany you on your journey. The** *ACE* **discribed the route looking out of the window travelling from Waterloo — westward, what could seen on the right was printed in red and that on the left was in blue. A large fold-out map was provided in the back of the book, showing towns, rivers and mileage.**

Above: **Bulleid Light Pacific No 34006** *Bude*, **wearing extended smoke deflectors, stands at the head of a West of England express at Waterloo on 17 June 1948. No 34006 was sent to the Highland section of the former LMS network to take part in that year's Locomotive Exchanges, being seen here attached to the Stanier LMS tender that enabled it to take advantage of the water troughs on that section. Water troughs were unknown on the Southern.** *J. H. Aston*

Below: **A wartime view of new 'Merchant Navy' No 21C7** *Aberdeen Commonwealth* **leaving Waterloo for Exeter Central with a train of 16 Maunsell carriages on 25 April 1942. The locomotive is in dirty black and is carrying its original heavily raked smoke-deflectors. The 'widow's peak' air vent in front of the chimney was not a success, as it caused smoke drift.** *Author's collection*

The 'Devon Belle'

Born of a desire to return to normality after years of wartime austerity, the 'Devon Belle' was an all-new Pullman service introduced in the summer of 1947. Running from Waterloo to Ilfracombe, it provided a First- and Third-class Pullman service and regularly included an observation car. It was also the first reservation-only train to operate in Britain.

The service began on 20 June 1947 and ran on Mondays, Fridays, Saturdays and Sundays. The down train left Waterloo at 12 noon, arriving at Exeter Central at 3.36pm and Ilfracombe at 5.32pm, while a separate portion of the train reached Plymouth Friary at 5.36pm. The return journey began with a departure from Plymouth Friary at 11.30am, the train arriving at Okehampton at 12.43pm and at Exeter Central at 1.27pm. The Ilfracombe service departed at 12 noon, arriving at Exeter Central at 1.38pm. The two portions were then attached, and the complete train departed at 1.40pm, reaching Waterloo at 5.20pm.

Between Waterloo and Exeter Central the regular motive power was a 'Merchant Navy' Pacific; west of Exeter Light Pacifics were used for the separate portions to Ilfracombe and Plymouth Friary.

In its early years the 'Devon Belle' was a great success, but a reduction in patronage saw the service removed from the timetable at the end of the 1954 summer season, the last train running on Saturday 18 September.

Right: **'Merchant Navy' No 35016** *Elders Fyffes* **heads the 'Devon Belle' through the cutting near Earlsfield in May 1949. The locomotive is painted in full Southern malachite green but has been fitted with a smokebox numberplate and has 'BRITISH RAILWAYS' in 'sunshine' lettering on the tender.** *S. V. Blencowe*

Centre right: **The all-Pullman 'Devon Belle', hauled by 'Merchant Navy' No 21C14** *Nederland Line*, **speeds through Raynes Park station on 26 September 1948.** *K. G. Carr*

Bellow right: **The 'Devon Belle' approaching Wilton in July 1947. 'Merchant Navy' No 21C16** *Elders Fyffes* **heads the train of newly painted and refurbished Pullman cars.** *R. S. Carpenter collection*

The DEVON BELLE

Fridays, Saturdays, Sundays and Mondays in each direction

dep 12.0 noon	Waterloo	arr 5.20 pm
arr 3.16 pm	Sidmouth Jct.	dep 2.3 pm
arr 3.36 pm	Exeter Ctl.	dep 1.40 pm
arr 5.32 pm	Ilfracombe	dep 12.0 noon
arr 5.36 pm	Plymouth Friary	dep 11.30 am

NEW!

ALL-PULLMAN TRAIN TO THE WEST OF ENGLAND

with Observation Car

SOUTHERN RAILWAY & PULLMAN CAR COMPANY

Left: **A changeover of 'Merchant Navy' Pacifics at Wilton in June 1952. Having brought the train from Waterloo, No 35011** *General Steam Navigation* **stands in the siding as No 35009** *Shaw Savill* **waits to depart for Exeter.** *R. Russell*

Below: **'Merchant Navy' No 35008** *Orient Line* **at speed with the 'Devon Belle' near Wilton South in August 1949. The locomotive is painted in the new BR livery.** *Brian Reed*

Right: **Approaching Seaton Junction on 8 September 1949, 'Merchant Navy' No 35005** *Canadian Pacific*, **in grubby malachite green, hauls an immaculate set of 13 Pullmans forming the up 'Devon Belle'.** *M. Whitehouse collection*

Below right: **Bulleid Light Pacific No 21C117** *Ilfracombe* **with the up 'Devon Belle' at Exeter St Davids** *circa* **July 1947. Note the mixed set of LMS and GWR carriages on the centre road, presumably from a through holiday train from the Midlands or the North of England.** *Author's collection*

Above: **The full 10-carriage formation of the up 'Devon Belle', seen near Umberleigh on 22 August 1949 with Bulleid Light Pacific No 34017** *Ilfracombe* **at its head.** *M. Whitehouse collection*

Below: **The down train seen later the same day near Barnstaple steaming through the hills on its way to Ilfracombe.** *M. Whitehouse collection*

Above: **Making its way slowly towards Barnstaple Junction station on 2 September 1949, the up 'Devon Belle' crosses the River Tor behind Bulleid Light Pacific No 34041** *Wilton*. *M. Whitehouse collection*

Left: **The 'Devon Belle' observation car being turned on the turntable at Ilfracombe in the summer of 1952. This photograph shows the body design and the paintwork, with its distinctive lettering, in detail.** *R. Russell*

Motive power and rolling stock

Locomotives

From the days of the 11am train in the LSWR period there was a policy of providing the best and most modern locomotives to haul this most important express. From the train's inception in the May 1890 timetable the motive power consisted of top-link Adams 4-4-0 tender engines of the 'T3', 'T6' and 'X6' classes. West of Exeter these were supplemented on the through service to Bude and Padstow by smaller Adams 4-4-0s such as the '460s'. The 'T3s' and 'T6s' were replaced in the late 1890s by Drummond 4-4-0s, primarily 'T9s' but also 'S11s' and 'L12s', prior to the introduction of the Drummond 4-6-0s, of which the 'F13', 'E14', 'P14' and 'T14' classes were all used on the service in the early 1900s. At around the same time the smaller '460s' gave way to Drummond's 'C8', 'K10' and 'L11' 4-4-0s, which continued to be the principal types in north Devon and Cornwall until the mid-1920s.

In the last years of LSWR operation the Urie 'N15' 4-6-0s became the mainstay of the Waterloo–Exeter service, and these, along with the later 'King Arthurs', continued to be used well into Southern Railway days, supplemented when necessary by the mixed-traffic 'S15' 4-6-0s, which could give a good turn of speed and performance. From 1925 Moguls of Classes N, N1, U and U1 were a common sight on the lines west of Exeter, often hauling portions of the 'Atlantic Coast Express' west of Okehampton to Bude and Padstow.

Perhaps surprisingly, World War 2 saw the introduction of Bulleid's new 'Merchant Navy' Pacifics, the first of which appeared in 1941, and these fine if sometimes temperamental machines would be the mainstay of the service from Waterloo to Exeter until the demise of the 'Atlantic Coast Express' in 1964. Bulleid's 'West Country' Light Pacifics, introduced from 1944, were also used on the 'Atlantic Coast Express' and 'Devon Belle' all the way from Waterloo when a 'Merchant Navy' was not available.

The postwar situation, with its austerity and restrictions, had a knock-on effect for services like the 'Atlantic Coast Express',

not least because it was difficult for the railway companies to obtain good coal for the locomotives. During 1947 the Southern Railway carried out extensive experiments with oil-burning locomotives to try to overcome the problem of poor coal; and members of several classes were converted for this project, including some Bulleid Light Pacifics, some Maunsell Moguls, and Drummond 4-4-0s of a number of classes including 'T9s', 'L12s' and 'D15s'. As a result of the increase in the price of oil, these experiments were curtailed in 1948, by which time supplies of good quality deep-mined coal were once again becoming readily available. But as a result of this situation in 1947 the lack of good coal took its toll on this once-proud express service to the West of England, and initially even the new Bulleid Pacifics could not improve timings after six years of war. However, after years of austerity, with dull black locomotives, dull green carriage stock and no restaurant cars, the splash of colour provided by the new Bulleid 'Merchant Navy' and Light Pacifics in bright malachite green hauling their equally bright rakes of new Bulleid corridor stock was a sight to behold.

After nationalisation on 1 January 1948 things would change little for the first two years of the existence of British Railways, but in the early 1950s came the introduction of first the BR Standard Class 3 2-6-2 tanks and, later, the Class 4 2-6-4 tanks, which worked portions of the 'Atlantic Coast Express' west of Okehampton on the Bude and Padstow lines. Meanwhile the Plymouth portion — and sometimes that to Ilfracombe — was often worked by a Standard Class 5 4-6-0 in lieu of a Bulleid Light Pacific. Even in the early 1960s, however, some services on the Bude and Padstow lines were still worked by the last surviving 'T9' 4-4-0s and sometimes an 'M7' 0-4-4 tank.

In 1964, the last year of the 'Atlantic Coast Express', the Western Region introduced 'Hymek' diesel-hydraulics on the services from Exeter Central to Ilfracombe and Plymouth, to supplement the steam diagrams over the same routes using traditional Southern motive power.

Left: **Drummond 'T7' 'Double Single' 4-2-2 No 720 heads a West of England express through Clapham Cutting *c*1906. The train is made up of non-corridor 48ft bogie stock with a six-wheel full-brake parcels van at the front. The Double Singles were not a great success on passenger or fast parcels and milk trains, and all were withdrawn soon after the Grouping in 1923.** *SLS collection*

Carriage stock

In the early days of the 11am service the train of non-corridor stock consisted largely of Panter 48ft bogie carriages, with long-wheelbase six-wheel non-corridor carriages and luggage vans as required. This improved in the early 1900s with the introduction of Surrey Warner corridor stock and dining cars which greatly improved the service for both First- and Third-class passengers, and made for a highly civilised journey to the South West. As the motive power was largely Drummond 4-4-0 and 4-6-0 locomotives, a large formation of from eight to 10 carriages would be used, depending on demand and on the motive power available. The stock was arranged to allow for through carriages to be detached at all points west of Salisbury and Exeter.

In Southern Railway days the composition of the train changed further with the introduction in the mid-1920s of Maunsell steel-bodied stock. Formations of this stock had to take into account through working to the train's numerous destinations before Exeter; this called for some careful planning by the operating department, as the same formation had to be reassembled by degrees on the journey back to Waterloo.

Towards the end of World War 2 new Bulleid-designed steel-bodied bogie stock began to appear, improving the overall comfort and quality of the service, and this was enhanced further by the introduction in the late 1940s of new dining and buffet cars. However, the 'Tavern' cars introduced in 1949 (and named as though they were inns or public houses) left much to be desired and were not popular with the travelling public; the original design, with its imitation brickwork and half-timbered upper portions, made the interiors dark and dingy, giving passengers the impression that they were travelling in a mobile dungeon, and the cars were later rebuilt in a more acceptable form.

In the late 1950s the Southern Region introduced sets of BR Mk 1 bogie stock, and these continued in use until the train's demise in 1964.

Right: **Drummond 'L12' 4-4-0 No 424 runs through Earlsfield station *c*1912 with a down West of England express made up of Surrey Warner corridor stock.**
SLS collection

Below: **Drummond 'T14' 4-6-0 No 446 speeds through Esher station *c*1907 with a train of Surrey Warner bogie carriage stock forming a Waterloo–Plymouth service. The 'T14' has a cross-tube firebox, a type that was fitted to many Drummond-designed locomotives at this time; however, these fireboxes were very demanding to maintain and were not a success, being removed during World War 1 by Robert Urie, Drummond's successor as Locomotive Superintendent.**
Ian Allan Library

Left: **Drummond 'L12' 4-4-0 No 419 heads a West of England train of 48ft non-corridor stock near Honiton** *c*1910. **These locomotives were often used on the London–West of England semi-fast and stopping services at this time but were later replaced by Drummond 4-6-0s.** *Ian Allan Library*

Right: **Adams '460' 4-4-0 No 526 passes Meldon Quarry with a train of LSWR non-corridor bogie stock on its way to Bude** *c*1919. **These locomotives were used on the services from Exeter Queen Street over the network of lines in north Devon and Cornwall until the late 1920s.** *SLS collection*

Below: **New Maunsell 'King Arthur' 4-6-0 No 776** *Sir Galagars* **passes through Walton-on-Thames with a down West of England express** *c*1925. **Without smoke-deflectors, the locomotive is seen as delivered by the North British Locomotive Co. Note the mixed rake of carriage stock in the train.** *SLS collection*

Above: **A rare view of a rebuilt Drummond 'T14' 4-6-0 on a West of England train, London-bound at Brookwood, c1938. Most of the 4-6-0s designed by Dugald Drummond in the 1900s failed to live up to their promise, but the 'T14s', albeit much modified, were kept in service until 1951. Note the signal gantry, which carries the LSWR pneumatic signalling equipment that could be found all the way from London to Basingstoke and lasted until the 1960s, when the Bournemouth line was electrified.** *R. Carpenter collection*

Right: **'N15' 4-6-0 No 451** *Sir Lamorak* **with a train of Surrey Warner corridor stock at Salisbury** *c*1926. **Note the dining car, third from the locomotive.** *SLS collection*

Left: **Bulleid Light Pacific No 21C112** *Launceston* **runs through Exmouth Junction with an up West of England express in the summer of 1946. The train is partly made up of Maunsell Open Third carriage stock.** *LCGB / Ken Nunn collection*

Above: **Nine Elms shed *c*1910, with a variety of Drummond 4-4-0s being prepared for various duties. This view shows the shed in its turn-of-the-century condition with the Drummond-era buildings.**
SLS collection

Right: **A view of Nine Elms shed in the early 1930s, showing the rebuilt buildings with their new roof, and the concrete-and-steel 'cenotaph' coal stage on the right. Among the locomotives on shed are Drummond 'K10' 4-4-0 No 145 and Urie 'H15' 4-6-0 No 489, while standing at the coal stage is an unidentified Maunsell 'King Arthur' 4-6-0.** *Roger Carpenter*

Left: **On 30 May 1931 Maunsell 'King Arthur' 4-6-0 No E785 *Sir Mador de la Porte* stands at the coal stage at Nine Elms shed as the driver completes an inspection before making the short journey to Waterloo.**
H. C. Casserley

Right: **During the summer months Salisbury shed provided motive power, in the form of changeover locomotives at Wilton, for both the 'ACE' and the 'Devon Belle'. 'King Arthur' No 30448** *Sir Tristram*, **freshly outshopped in Bulleid malachite green, stands in Salisbury shed yard during August 1948. Note the transitional livery, fully lined but with 'BRITISH RAILWAYS' lettering in Gill Sans on the tender.** *F. Foote*

Above: **A broadside view of No 30448 at Salisbury shed yard in August 1948, showing all the detail of the livery.** *F. Foote*

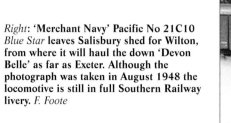

Right: **'Merchant Navy' Pacific No 21C10** *Blue Star* **leaves Salisbury shed for Wilton, from where it will haul the down 'Devon Belle' as far as Exeter. Although the photograph was taken in August 1948 the locomotive is still in full Southern Railway livery.** *F. Foote*

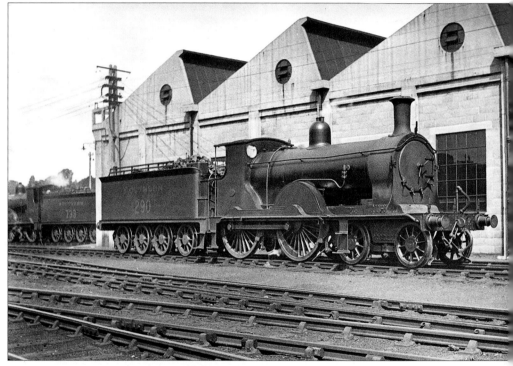

Above: **A bird's-eye view of the locomotive yard at Exmouth Junction shed on 29 June 1948, with Bulleid Light Pacific No S21C107** *Wadebridge* **in the foreground and behind it No 21C125** *Whimple* **(formerly** *Rough Tor*)**, surrounded by various locomotives of Maunsell or Drummond design.** *J. H. Aston*

Right: **Exmouth Junction was the home of the banking locomotives that worked on the heavily graded section of line between Exeter Central and St Davids. The first standard class of locomotives used on this duty were the 'E1/R' 0-6-2Ts, which appeared in 1927 as rebuilds of Stroudley LBSCR 'E1' 0-6-0T locomotives. One of them, No 2096, is seen here in newly rebuilt condition at Eastleigh Works yard** *c*1927**. The 'E1/Rs' were also used on the North Devon & Cornwall Junction Railway.** *Author's collection*

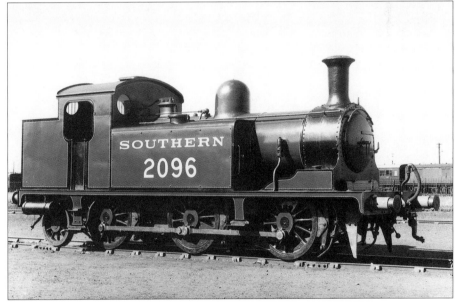

Left: **'Z'-class 0-8-0T No 958 at Exmouth Junction** *c*1935**. These plain but impressive locomotives, eight of which were built, in 1929, were designed for heavy shunting in yards and later in their careers were employed on banking duties at Exeter, where, having replaced the 'E1/R' 0-6-2Ts, they remained in use until late 1962.** *Author's collection*

Above: **Plymouth Friary shed** *c*1925, with Maunsell 'N'-class Mogul No 1827 and an unidentified Drummond 'T9' 4-4-0 in the yard. The building, which is a typical small Drummond-era locomotive shed from the early 20th century, appears to be in very good condition and well maintained. *SLS collection*

Below: **Plymouth Friary** photographed from the same spot 29 years later, in June 1954, with three 'M7' 0-4-4Ts on shed. The front of the building is now sheeted in corrugated iron, which has replaced the glass front window; and the original small vents have been removed. *Photomatic*

Above: **Plymouth Friary shed *c*1955, with a Bulleid Light Pacific being serviced. Locomotives of this class were allocated here from the late 1940s until the early '50s, when they were transferred to Exmouth Junction.** *SLS collection*

Below: **Plymouth Friary on 5 May 1963, towards the end of its existence, with rebuilt Bulleid Light Pacific No 34036 *Westward Ho* on shed and a Maunsell 'N'-class Mogul behind the building on the left.** *S. C. Nash / SLS collection*

Left: Barnstaple shed often provided motive power for the 'ACE' on the Ilfracombe–Exeter section of the journey. On 21 July 1925 'A12' ('Jubilee') 0-4-2 No E628 and Maunsell 'N'-class Mogul No A860 simmer on shed while awaiting their next turn of duty. *H. C. Casserley*

Below: Barnstaple shed in the summer of 1952, with 'M7' 0-4-4T No 30253 and an unidentified 'E1/R' 0-6-2T standing in the yard. *Author's collection*

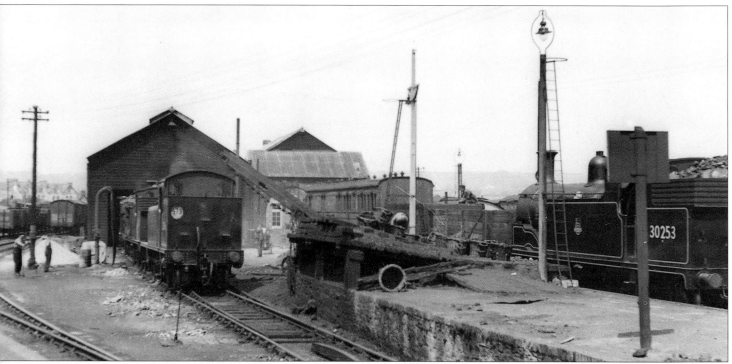

Left: The two-road timber locomotive shed at Barnstaple on 5 June 1960, with an Ivatt '2MT' 2-6-2T simmering inside. The ex-LSWR Surrey Warner bogie brake carriage on the far right is a Departmental vehicle, recently repainted and overhauled. *S. C. Nash / SLS collection*

Right: **Wadebridge shed *c*1925, with Beattie well tanks on shed — No E0329 outside and No E0314 behind. 'A12' ('Jubilee') 0-4-2 No E629 stands just outside the shed near the locomotive hoist. Like the shed at Barnstaple, the building dates from the Adams era. On the far right a Beattie-era carriage body survives as an office.**
SLS collection

Below: **Wadebridge shed *circa* June 1936: a view in the opposite direction, towards the water tower and coal stage. Simmering in the yard is a Beattie well tank, while standing on shed are a pair of Maunsell 'N'-class Moguls.** *SLS collection*

A journey on the 'ACE'

The 'Atlantic Coast Express' was one of Britain's most successful and, in summer, most heavily used trains; at the height of the summer season the train often had up to 13 carriages bound for seven destinations — Sidmouth, Exmouth, Ilfracombe, Torrington, Plymouth, Bude and Padstow.

Waterloo station is one of the most impressive and beautiful stations in London. This spacious and well-appointed terminus was designed by Alfred Weeks Szlumper, the resident engineer of the LSWR, and J. R. Scott, the chief assistant architect for the LSWR. (A. W. Szlumper was father of Sir Gilbert Szlumper, for a short time General Manager of the Southern Railway.) The original ramshackle station that had existed from the late 1840s had been extended over the decades until the early 1890s, when it became inadequate for the operational needs; but work had to be suspended during World War 1, and the new station was not opened until 1922. Our journey, in the autumn of 1959, will begin from under the impressive steel and glass roof that covers most of the impressive structure.

The train's consist changed over the period of the service's existence, as the 'Atlantic Coast Express' normally had the most modern rolling stock available. Today we have a train of 12 carriages in our formation, which a Drummond 'M7' 0-4-4 tank has just brought in from Clapham Yard. The train consists of an SK (standard corridor) and a BCK (brake composite corridor) for Ilfracombe, a BCK for Torrington, a BCK for Padstow, a BCK for Bude, a two-coach set — comprising a BSK (brake standard corridor) and a BCK — for Plymouth, a two-car dining set comprising an RKB (restaurant kitchen buffet) and an RCO (restaurant composite open) (both to be detached at Exeter), a BCK for Exmouth, a BCK for Sidmouth (both to be detached at

Below: **Under the clock at Waterloo in the summer of 1948, in the immediate postwar austerity period before any refurbishment had taken place. A crowd of holidaymakers queue behind the appropriate boards, ready to join the 'ACE' for their long journey to the beaches of the South West.** *Ian Allan Library*

Sidmouth Junction) and finally a BCK for Honiton (to be detached at Salisbury).

There is a feeling of anticipation as the hands of the clock approach 11am and the crew of our rebuilt Bulleid 'Merchant Navy' prepare for departure. As we start, the mighty green-painted mass of the Pacific slips to a standstill with a thundering roar, but then finds its feet as it eases the long train out across the labyrinth of tracks, crossings and pointwork. We are ably assisted at the rear by the 'M7' until we are halfway to Vauxhall, where, its work done, the Drummond tank drops behind, leaving us to continue our long journey to the far South West of England.

The 'Merchant Navy' has taken up its train and now gets into a pace of its own as we pass Vauxhall and on towards Nine Elms, where the shed and former LSWR works on the left are full of locomotives being prepared and disposed of after their duties. On the right we can see the extensive goods yard, which includes the original LSWR terminus buildings dating from 1838.

Soon we pass the looming, tall shape of Battersea power station, and the GWR's South Lambeth goods depot, and then pass under the two overbridges that carry the former London, Chatham & Dover main lines from Victoria to the Kent coast, and also the south London suburban line of the LBSCR, before we pass through Queen's Road, Battersea (now called Queenstown Road); then almost immediately we pass under a third overbridge, which carries the ex-LBSCR lines from Victoria to the South Coast, then run parallel on our left as far as Clapham Junction station.

We are now out in the middle of Clapham Junction, with main lines on either side of us. Our train is slowly gathering speed as we approach Clapham Junction station. To our right we can see the West London line from Kensington Olympia and north-west London; on the left are the South Coast lines to Brighton and Eastbourne. We pass through Clapham Junction station with its extensive platforms on the South Western and Brighton lines, under Concert Hall Bridge and through into Clapham Cutting;

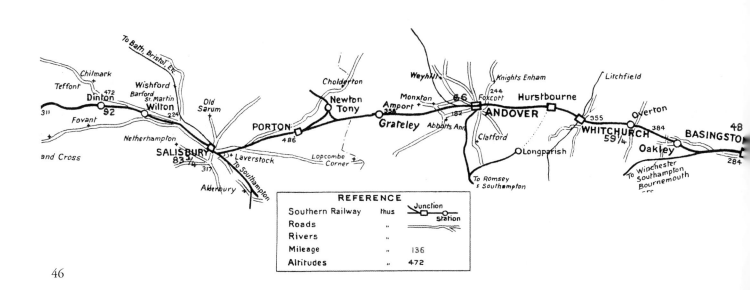

Above left: Nearing Vauxhall, 'Merchant Navy' No 35028 *Clan Line* heads a train of mixed Maunsell and Bulleid stock forming a West of England express *c*1963. *P. H. Groom*

Left: A very dirty rebuilt Bulleid Light Pacific No 34108 *Wincanton* approaches Vauxhall station *c*1961, with a West of England semi-fast. Note the amount of high-rise development going on in the background. *P. H. Groom*

Above: Rebuilt 'Merchant Navy' No 35029 *Ellerman Lines* runs through Vauxhall station on the 'ACE' in the summer of 1962 with a long train of Bulleid bogie stock. The buildings on the far left have since been replaced by a high-rise block of government offices. *David Knapman*

Below: Rebuilt Bulleid Light Pacific No 34054 *Lord Beaverbrook* with the London-bound 'ACE' passes through Clapham Junction station in the winter of 1962. Note the unidentified Bulleid Light Pacific in the background and the Bulleid Bournemouth set on the right. *Keith Harwood*

then we reach Earlsfield station, with Durnsford Road power station and the Wimbledon carriage depot on the right. We can also observe at this point the District Line on its approach to its terminus at Wimbledon station. Running from Wimbledon via Putney to Waterloo, this had been the first LSWR's electrified line, opening in 1915.

Now through Wimbledon, we continue south, past the Wimbledon signal works and the lines to Croydon and Sutton. We are heading through Raynes Park station — junction for the lines to Epsom and Chessington — with suburban housing on each side, and soon reach New Malden — junction for the line to Kingston — and on to Surbiton, where we speed through on the centre tracks and continue south under the bridge that takes the flying junction for the lines to Hampton Court. On the left we can also see the junction for the lines to Guildford and Shepperton.

We are soon through Esher, and pass Sandown Park racecourse on the left. We now run through the fast centre tracks at Hersham and a few minutes later reach Walton-on-Thames. The next station we pass through is Weybridge, with its junction for Virginia Water and the Reading line on the right. Soon after Weybridge we pass the banking of the former Brooklands motor-racing circuit. The part of the Brooklands site on our left is now a factory for Vickers-Armstrong, the aircraft manufacturer. We pass through West Weybridge (now called Byfleet & New Haw) and continue on to Byfleet (now West Byfleet), where we start a climb for 10 miles at 1 in 314 to Milepost 31, just beyond Brookwood.

We speed through Woking, with its junction for Guildford and Portsmouth on the left and its extensive goods and engineers' yards on each side. Next comes Brookwood station, which had

Above: **Bulleid Light Pacific No 34099** *Lynmouth* **hurries the relief 'ACE' through Clapham Cutting on its way to Earlsfield on 11 October 1958. The locomotive still has a tender in its original high-sided condition.** *P. H. Groom*

Above right: **Bulleid Light Pacific No 34080** *74 Squadron* **runs through Clapham Cutting with an up West of England train on 22 August 1964. This locomotive also has a high-sided tender but has recently had an overhaul and repaint which has included the application of the later (1956) totem.** *P. H. Groom*

Right: **'H15' 4-6-0 No 30521 nears Earlsfield with the 11.54am Salisbury train on 25 July 1959. By this time even the Maunsell-built 'H15s' were being withdrawn, culminating in the extinction of the class by the end of 1961.** *J. C. Beckett*

once been the junction for branches to, on our right, the National Rifle Association's camp at Bisley (the branch closing in 1952), and, on our left, Brookwood Cemetery, owned by the London Necropolis Company and closed to traffic in 1941 after the company's station at Waterloo was bombed.

At Pirbright Junction the lines from Aldershot and Alton connect to the South Western main line on the left and right. We now pass under the Basingstoke Canal, which is carried across the South Western main line on a brick aqueduct, and through the triangular junction where the lines from Ascot come in on our right. Heading from Surrey into Hampshire, we cross over the Reading–Tonbridge line and then pass through Farnborough Main station 33 miles from London, on the centre running roads. On our left we can see the coal-yard sidings with a connecting line to the Royal Aircraft Establishment, which has its own internal railway system, constructed during World War 1 by German prisoners of war.

Above: **Wimbledon EMU depot** *c*1953, with an interesting selection of early electric units in the storage sidings in front of the depot. '**N15' No 30449** *Sir Torre*, with an up West of England train, is chased by a Maunsell '4-SUB' unit descending from the flyover. *A. A. Sellman*

Below right: **H15' 4-6-0 No 30524 coasts past Wimbledon 'B' signalbox to stop in the station with an afternoon Basingstoke–Waterloo train on 16 July 1959. Note the unkempt condition of the locomotive, contrasting with the clean set of green Bulleid bogie stock. The Wimbledon signal works can be seen in the background.** *J. C. Beckett*

Right: Bulleid Light Pacific No 34106 *Lydford* heads a West of England express made up of BR Mk 1 and Bulleid stock south of Wimbledon station, heading towards Raynes Park on 4 August 1964. Note (left) the Bulleid '4-SUB' unit, heading towards Wimbledon, and (right) the coal yard full of wagons. *Author's collection*

Below: A modern-day Health & Safety officer's nightmare: Bulleid Light Pacific No 34061 *73 Squadron* roars past Raynes Park with a fast West of England train on 27 September 1959. One hopes for the photographer's sake that there were no trains coming in the opposite direction. *J. H. Aston*

Bottom: 'Merchant Navy' No 35016 *Elders Fyffes* passes New Malden on 2 March 1963 with the down 'ACE'. This photograph shows the locomotive in immaculate condition with a rake of equally clean Bulleid carriages. *B. Wadey*

Above: 'Merchant Navy' No 35007 *Aberdeen Commonwealth*, in BR blue livery, heads a 13-carriage train towards Surbiton station *c*1951. Note the interesting contrast in liveries, some stock being still in malachite green and other vehicles in carmine-and-cream. *Author's collection*

Below: A contrasting scene from eight years later: rebuilt 'Merchant Navy' No 35029 *Ellerman Lines* approaches the same spot with the down 'ACE' on 16 October 1959. As in the previous photograph, the locomotive and its train are in immaculate condition, befitting the importance of this fast West of England service. *J. C. Beckett*

Above: **Bulleid Light Pacific No 34065** *Hurricane* **roars along the centre road at Surbiton station on 5 September 1959 with a through West of England train consisting mostly of Maunsell stock.**
Author's collection

Below: **Rebuilt Bulleid Light Pacific No 34009** *Lyme Regis* **passes Hersham with the 3pm Waterloo–Exeter on 5 September 1964, the last day of regular steam working on the West of England main line. The message chalked on the smokebox door reads 'STEAM FOREVER'.**
B. Wadey

Above: The pioneer of the 'Merchant Navy' class, No 35001 *Channel Packet*, waits to depart Woking with a Waterloo–Exeter semi-fast on 23 August 1964. The locomotive and train are oily but otherwise clean. *B. Wadey*

Below: Bulleid Light Pacific No 34057 *Biggin Hill* passes Woking with the down relief 'ACE' — the 10.35am from Waterloo to Exeter, Padstow and Bude — on 25 July 1964. This train is a mixture of Bulleid and BR Mk 1 carriage stock. *B. Wadey*

Above: 'Merchant Navy' No 35030 *Elder Dempster Line*s passes Brookwood with the down 'ACE' in December 1963, passing Bulleid Light Pacific No 34071 *601 Squadron*, which is hauling the 10.54am Waterloo–Salisbury stopping train on the slow line. *G. Siviour*

Right: 'Merchant Navy' No 35014 *Nederland Line* heads through Brookwood *c*1962 with the down 'ACE'. The formation is of particular interest, comprising a mixture of Maunsell Restriction 1, Bulleid and BR Mk 1 carriage stock. *Author's collection*

Below: Bulleid Light Pacific No 34019 *Bideford* passes Pirbright Junction *c*1954 with a West of England express consisting of Bulleid and Maunsell stock. The buildings in the background are railway workers' cottages. *W. Gilburt*

Above: 'Merchant Navy' No 35009 *Shaw Savill* enters Deepcut Cutting *c*1963, with the 3pm Waterloo–West of England train. *J. C. Beckett*

Below: Rebuilt Bulleid Light Pacific No 34058 *Sir Frederick Pile* in Deepcut Cutting with the up 'ACE' on 29 August 1961. The train consists of Maunsell, Bulleid and BR Mk 1 stock, including a restaurant car second from the locomotive. *J. C. Beckett*

Continuing south from Farnborough, we pass through Fleet and Winchfield stations before reaching Hook. After Milepost 42 we begin making our approach into Basingstoke, where, as we emerge from the long cutting on the approach to the South Western station, we can see on our right the junction with the Great Western line from Reading. Basingstoke is 48 miles from London. This important market town once had a connecting line south to Alton; this was opened as a light railway in 1900 but was closed by the Southern in 1935. By now the only remains of this line at Basingstoke are a section the headshunt leading down to the Thornycroft motor works south of the station and a bay platform (still known as the Alton bay) on the down side. During our journey from Wimbledon to this point on the quadrupled main line we have been controlled by the automatic pneumatic semaphore signalling system installed by LSWR during the last decade of its existence.

Still running south and now on the level, we soon reach Battledown Viaduct with its flyover, the last on the main line from Waterloo. We pass under the main line to Southampton and Bournemouth and continue on our way passing Oakley, Overton and Whitchurch. Soon after Whitchurch we cross the Didcot, Newbury & Southampton line before reaching Hurstbourne, 61 miles from London.

Having crossed the River Anton, we shortly reach Andover Junction, which has a branch running south to Southampton, which we can see on the left. After passing through Andover Junction we soon reach Redpost Junction, where, on the right, the tracks of the Midland & South Western Junction Railway run north to Swindon and Cheltenham. West of Redpost Junction we pass through Grateley, with its connecting branch to Bulford, and cross the Hampshire/Wiltshire border just north of Idmiston Halt. Shortly afterwards we pass Porton, which serves the Chemical Weapons Research Establishment at Porton Down.

Continuing west, we pass Fisherton Junction, head through Fisherton Tunnel and cross the River Avon before our first scheduled stop of the day at Salisbury, 85 miles from London. Here the BCK is detached and added to a stopping train, nominally for Honiton, although it will in fact continue as far as Exeter Central. At Salisbury too our locomotive has to take on water, there being no troughs on the Southern. While we wait in the station the fireman moves the coal forward to the front of the tender.

Salisbury originally had two stations — one for the LSWR and, alongside it, the terminus of the GWR's line from Westbury. However, during the 1930s the Southern came to an agreement with the Great Western under which the latter's trains were allowed to use the Southern's stations at Salisbury and Basingstoke, improving the economic operation of services in both places.

Above right: **Bulleid Light Pacific No 34078** *222 Squadron* **restarts the 12.58pm Salisbury–Waterloo stopping train from Farnborough on 22 September 1961. Note the gantry, with the LSWR pneumatic signals still in use.** *B. Wadey*

Right: **'Merchant Navy' No 35002** *Union Castle*, **still with its original high-sided tender, speeds the up 'ACE' through Fleet station** *c*1952. **The stock is a mixture of Bulleid and Maunsell vehicles, including a Maunsell restaurant car.** *C. M. and J. M. Bentley collection*

Above: **Rebuilt 'Merchant Navy' No 35014** *Nederland Line* **in Winchfield Cutting with the down 'ACE' on 13 August 1960. In the background is one of the pneumatic-signal gantries that were found between Brookwood and Basingstoke.** *J. C. Beckett*

Below: **'King Arthur' 4-6-0 No 30798** *Sir Hectimere*, **still with its six-wheel tender from its days on the Kent coast, heads an up West of England express under the road viaduct at Winchfield Cutting on 13 August 1960.** *J. C. Beckett*

Right: **Rebuilt Bulleid Light Pacific No 34059** *Sir Archibald Sinclair* **passes Winchfield station with the 10.45pm down West of England express from Waterloo on 13 August 1960. Note the fine array of pneumatic signals.** *J. C. Beckett*

Below: **Bulleid Light Pacific No 34109** *Sir Trafford Leigh-Mallory* **takes an up West of England express at speed through Hook on 13 September 1959. The train is made up of Bulleid and Maunsell stock. The dining car is the third vehicle from the locomotive. Note the railway workers' cottages on the right.** *B. Wadey*

Left: 'King Arthur' 4-6-0 No 30782 *Sir Brian* in the cutting east of Basingstoke with an up West of England express on 1 September 1962. The locomotive has an LSWR-type bogie tender and is hauling a mixed rake of Bulleid, Maunsell and BR Mk 1 stock, including a BR Mk 1 restaurant car (sixth in the formation). Within three months all remaining members of the 'King Arthur' class would be withdrawn. *J. C. Beckett*

Below left: 'Lord Nelson' 4-6-0 No 30861 *Lord Anson* approaches Basingstoke *en route* from Waterloo to Exeter with the Southern Counties Touring Society 'South Western Limited' special of 2 September 1962. Like the 'Arthurs', all the surviving 'Lord Nelson' locomotives would be withdrawn from service by the end of 1962. *B. Wadey*

Below: On 4 September 1964 rebuilt Bulleid Light Pacific No 34095 *Brentor* stands with its Bournemouth-line train at the fast platform at Basingstoke while No 34046 *Braunton* runs through with a West of England express. *C. M. and J. M. Bentley collection*

Above right: Bulleid Light Pacific No 34002 *Salisbury* approaches Basingstoke on 25 July 1964 with the 10.28am Exeter–Waterloo train, comprising a mixture of Bulleid and BR Mk 1 stock. *B. Wadey*

Below right: On 25 July 1964 Bulleid Light Pacific No 34064 *Fighter Command* leaves Basingstoke with the 3pm Waterloo–Exeter train, running more than 30 minutes late. *B. Wadey*

Above: **'Britannia' Pacific No 70020** *Mercury* **dives under Battledown Flyover, heading for Salisbury with the South Western Ramblers' excursion on 3 March 1964. This rare portrait of a 'Britannia' working on the Southern depicts the fine lines of this well-crafted class of locomotive.** *J. C. Beckett*

Left: **Maunsell 'S15' No 30832 thunders under Battledown Flyover with an up West of England train on 9 August 1952. The 'S15s' were normally used on goods services, mostly out of Feltham Yard, but were often employed on passenger services in the summer months when a suitable passenger locomotive was not available.** *R. E. Wilson*

Below left: **Bulleid Light Pacific No 34039** *Boscastle* **hurries under Battledown Flyover with a down West of England express in the summer of 1963.** *Mike Esau*

Above right: **With the sun glinting on its boiler and tender, 'Lord Nelson' No 30856** *Lord St Vincent* **leaves Andover with the 4.5pm Salisbury–Waterloo stopping train on 30 March 1959. These large and impressive 4-6-0s, introduced by the Southern Railway in 1926, were a common sight on trains from Salisbury to London in the late 1950s and early 1960s.** *B. Wadey*

Right: **Rebuilt 'Merchant Navy' No 35018** *British India Line* **passes Andover Junction with the down 'ACE' on 30 March 1959. The connecting line from the Midland & South Western Junction Railway is visible in the distance.** *B. Wadey*

Above: 'King Arthur' 4-6-0 No 30774 *Sir Gaheris* approaches Whitchurch on 18 July 1958 with the 3.15pm Salisbury–Waterloo semi-fast. The train is made up of Maunsell, Bulleid and BR Mk 1 stock. *B. Wadey*

Left: Whitchurch in May 1965, with Bulleid Light Pacific No 34007 *Wadebridge* at the head of an up stopping train and the LSWR steel footbridge in the background. *P. H. Groom*

Left: The other end of Whitchurch station, pictured *c*1963, with the 'ACE' headed by 'Merchant Navy' No 35030 *Elder Dempster Lines* running under the steel footbridge. *Mike Esau*

Above: **Grateley station** *c*1964, **with rebuilt 'Merchant Navy' No 35024** *East Asiatic Company* **tearing through at the head of a West of England express. Note the goods yard, full of assorted coal wagons.** *E. T. Gill / R. K. Blencowe collection*

Below: **'Merchant Navy' No 35021** *East Asiatic Company* **stands at the platform at Salisbury with an up West of England train in the summer of 1951. By now a number of 'Merchant Navys' had variations in the style of the air-smoothed casing, and BR was starting to modify the tenders by removing the streamlined casing around the coal bunker to facilitate access for coaling and watering.** *Author's collection*

Above: **Ex-LMS Co-Co diesel No 10000 arrives at Salisbury with a down West of England express on 16 May 1953. At this time BR was testing and evaluating its small fleet of main-line diesels on various routes, among them the West of England main line; both the ex-LMS twins and the later Bulleid 1Co-Co1s were used on trials on the line during 1953.** *E. W. Fry / R. K. Blencowe collection*

Below: **Photographed from the same position, 'Merchant Navy' No 35017** *Belgian Marine* **is seen in charge of the down 'ACE' in the summer of 1960. In the intervening seven years there has been little or no change at the east end of Salisbury station; note once again the wartime signalbox, with its distinctive flat roof.** *David Johnson*

Above: **Bulleid Light Pacific No 34030** *Watersmeet* **starts a down semi-fast out of Salisbury station on 16 May 1964. The train is made up of Bulleid and BR Mk 1 stock. Note (left) the ex-GWR goods shed and yard in the background, dating back to the period when Salisbury had two stations.** *C. M. and J. M. Bentley collection*

Below: **New in 1941, 'Merchant Navy' No 35004** *Cunard White Star* **remains in its early air-smoothed condition as it leaves Salisbury with a West of England train in the summer of 1948. Note, however, the new BR number in Bulleid 'sunshine' lettering above the front buffer-beam.** *Author's collection*

We leave Salisbury's sharply curved platform heading west, climbing mostly at 1 in 115, and continue on our journey past the locomotive depot (on the left) on our way to Wilton, famous for its carpet factory.

Having passed over the River Wylye and through Dinton station, we cross the River Nadder to reach Tisbury, 96 miles from London. We pass over some tributaries of the Nadder before passing through Semley, on the Wiltshire/Dorset border. Here begins the amazing switchback of steep gradients for which this line is famous, which will cause our speed alternately to increase, as our locomotive charges downhill to get a run at the next bank, and then drop, as it blasts its way up to another summit.

We cross the River Loddon, and soon reach the market town of Gillingham, 105 miles from London, after which we cross the River Stour. It has been a sharp descent of 1 in 100 from Semley, but after the River Stour we begin a climb that culminates in a 1-in-100 bank shortly before Buckhorn Weston Tunnel. At the entrance to the tunnel the line sweeps downhill again at 1 in 100. The speed of the train reaches the 80s before, at the bottom of this dip, the line begins to climb again on a 1-in-100 gradient that brings us to Templecombe, at Milepost 113.

Templecombe is an important junction, the South Western main line crossing over the cross-country line of the former Somerset & Dorset Joint Railway, which carries through traffic to Bournemouth and the Midlands. The Southern station, on two levels, is located a little to the west of the S&D line and can be reached from the latter only by means of a spur which joins the South Western from the north.

After leaving Templecombe we continue west through Milborne Port, passing back into Dorset before reaching the market town of Sherborne. From here we continue south-west to Yeovil, crossing the River Yeo as we pass once more into Somerset. As we run through Yeovil Junction station, 123 miles from London, we cross over the Great Western line from Castle Cary to Weymouth.

Yeovil has three stations — Yeovil Junction (Southern), Yeovil Town (SR/GWR joint) and Yeovil Pen Mill (on the GWR main line to Weymouth) — connected by a local service. After leaving Yeovil Junction we cross the River Yeo again on the Dorset/Somerset border before reaching Sutton Bingham. Crossing the River Parrett, we run through another pocket of Dorset before returning to Somerset. Our train is now battling with three miles of 1-in-80 gradient to Crewkerne, famous for its weaving and sail-making; it was here that the sails for Nelson's *Victory* were made.

After leaving Crewkerne we have 13 miles of fast downhill running. Traversing the picturesque Axe Valley, we pass through Crewkerne Tunnel and cross the River Vine, re-entering Dorset for another short stretch before crossing back into Somerset.

Having passed Chard Junction, where the joint branch to Chard diverges on our right, we leaves Somerset for good and head into Devon. About two miles before Axminster station the railway is bridged by the ancient Fosse Way, the Roman road that ran all the way from Exeter to Lincoln via Ilchester, Bath, Cirencester and Leicester. Shortly afterwards we arrive at Axminster, the second carpet-making town on our route, 144 miles from London. Here, in the bay on the right, we see an Adams 4-4-2 radial tank engine waiting to depart for Lyme Regis with a train of ex-LSWR corridor stock.

West of Axminster we pass under the Lyme Regis branch, which crosses the line by means of an overbridge. Shortly afterwards we cross the River Axe before reaching Seaton Junction station, from which, on our left, a branch runs south to Seaton itself. A few minutes later we run through Honiton Tunnel, and then descend for nearly five miles at a gradient of almost 1 in 80, through Honiton station, over the River Otter, and on to Sidmouth Junction, 159 miles from London. This is the junction for the branch to Sidmouth and Exmouth, and two BCKs — one for each destination — are detached here before we continue westwards.

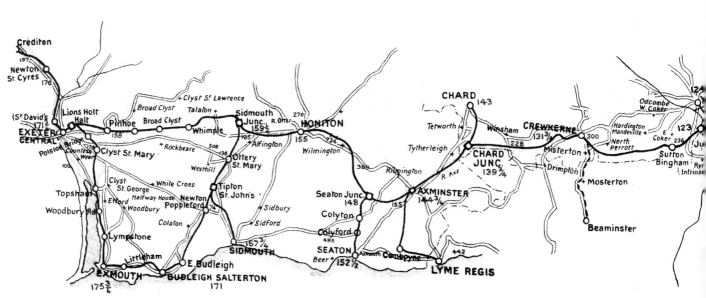

Above: **Passing Wilton with the up 'ACE' in the summer of 1951, 'Merchant Navy' No 35025** *Brocklebank Line*, **in the new BR blue livery, heads a train of Bulleid carriage stock in a mix of Southern malachite green and BR carmine-and-cream.** *R. K. Blencowe*

Right: **'Merchant Navy' No 35005** *Canadian Pacific* **passes through Tisbury station with a West of England train in the winter of 1963/4.** *E. T. Gill / R. K. Blencowe collection*

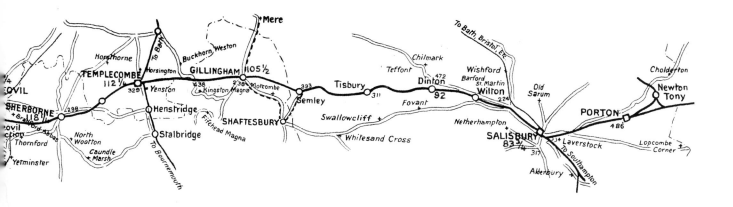

Left: Rebuilt 'Merchant Navy' No 35018 *British India Line* runs through Semley with the 'ACE' in the spring of 1961. Note the goods yard on the left. *Transport Treasury*

Below left: Templecombe station *c*1950, seen looking east from the signalbox and clearly showing the Walker-era buildings that replaced the original station during the 1930s. There was a connecting chord from here to the Somerset & Dorset line east of the station. *Lens of Sutton Association*

Bottom: The down 'ACE' west of Templecombe behind 'Merchant Navy' No 35030 *Elder Dempster Lines* in July 1963. The train is a mix of BR Mk 1 and Bulleid stock. *G. Siviour*

Above right: 'S15' 4-6-0 No 30823 waits at the platform at Yeovil Junction on 25 August 1962 with the 10.37am Exeter–Salisbury stopping train. Some of these locomotives — unlike the 'King Arthurs', the last of which were withdrawn at the end of 1962 — would remain in service until the autumn of 1965. *B. Wadey*

Right: Chard Junction in the summer of 1960, with Bulleid Light Pacific No 34092 *City of Wells* heading a westbound train through the station as station staff look on. This station was the junction for the line to Chard, which had a joint LSWR/GWR station. *E. T. Gill / R. K. Blencowe collection*

Left: **Rebuilt Bulleid Light Pacific No 34032** *Camelford* passes Chard Junction with an up express on 2 September 1961. Note the level crossing, the distinctive LSWR signalbox, the lattice signal-post with a Southern upper-quadrant arm, and the equally distinctive lattice footbridge in the background. *J. C. Beckett*

Below left: **Axminster in the summer of 1963 with an Ivatt 2-6-2 tank simmering in the bay platform for the Lyme Regis branch.** This photograph shows the distinctive footbridge with its enclosed roof, the attractive main station buildings and the large water tower, with its brick base. *R. K. Blencowe*

Right: **Adams radial 4-4-2T No 30584 leaves Axminster station with a single Maunsell corridor Brake Third in the winter of 1959.** In the background can be seen the main-line station, and on the far right the goods yard. Note the sharp incline of the branch leading up to the overbridge that carried the Lyme Regis line over the West of England main line. *J. A. Coiley*

Above: **A rare photograph, taken** *c*1960, **of Adams radial tanks double-heading a train on the Lyme Regis branch.** No 30583 heads No 30584. The train formation is also of interest, comprising BR Mk 1 stock in carmine-and-cream and two Bulleid vehicles in malachite green, a non-corridor 100-seater bringing up the rear. *Author's collection*

Right: **No 30584 crosses Cannington Viaduct with a Lyme Regis–Axminster train on 15 April 1960.** When constructed this viaduct suffered from subsidence, necessitating the addition of the 'jack arch' seen in this photograph. *J. C. Beckett*

Above: 'S15' No 30843 climbs Seaton Bank in the summer of 1958 with a five-car Bulleid set forming a West of England train. *Ian Allan Library*

Right: Bulleid Light Pacific No 34070 *Manston* leaves the platform at Seaton Junction with three BR Mk 1 carriages forming the 8.10am Ilfracombe train on 1 June 1963. Note the impressive array of LSWR lower-quadrant signals on their lattice posts. *J. H. Aston*

Left: The same location on 7 June 1963, with Bulleid Light Pacific No 34091 *Weymouth* heading a train of empty milk tankers. Such traffic was as important to the railway as the 'ACE' and was a familiar sight to passengers on fast expresses as they made their way towards Devon and Cornwall. *David Johnson*

Above: **Seaton Junction on 31 August 1957, with a local train headed by an 'M7' 0-4-4T waiting at the bay platform for the main-line train to Exeter. The Seaton branch (right) was a regular haunt of the 'M7' tanks.** *R. K. Blencowe*

Right: **'M7' No 30045 simmers in the bay platform at Seaton Junction after arriving with a train from Seaton on 17 August 1956. The long concrete footbridge in the background formed part of a public right of way across the station complex.** *C. M. and J. M. Bentley collection*

Right: **Rebuilt Bulleid Light Pacific No 34048** *Crediton* **runs up Honiton Bank and heads towards the tunnel with the 1pm Waterloo–West of England train on 16 April 1960.** *J. C. Beckett*

Above: **Rebuilt 'Merchant Navy' No 35028 *Clan Line* nears Honiton Tunnel with the 2.15pm Waterloo–West of England train on 4 August 1962.** *J. C. Beckett*

Left: **On 27 June 1960 'Merchant Navy' No 35004 *Cunard White Star* approaches Honiton Incline signalbox with the 1pm Waterloo–West of England train.** *J. C. Beckett*

Left: **Cresting the summit and about to enter Honiton Tunnel with the up 'ACE', 'Merchant Navy' No 35009 *Shaw Savill* heads its mixed train of 12 Bulleid and BR Mk 1 vehicles through the Devon hills in bright sunshine on 15 May 1964.** *J. C. Beckett*

Above: 'Merchant Navy' No 35010 *Blue Star* just east of Honiton Tunnel with the up 'ACE' in the summer of 1962. The dirty, oily look of the locomotive betokens a difficulty in recruiting cleaners at the time. *Mike Esau*

Right: Bulleid Light Pacific No 34018 *Axminster* bursts out of Honiton Tunnel with the 'ACE' on 3 August 1955. *R. K. Blencowe*

Below: 'Merchant Navy' No 35025 *Brocklebank Line* heads the 10.30am train to Exeter Central past Sidmouth Junction on 31 May 1963. An Ivatt 2-6-2T stands with the Sidmouth-branch train at the bay platform on the far left, and a Standard Class 4 2-6-0 simmers at the platform in the background. Note the distinctive tall LSWR signalbox on the right. *J. H. Aston*

Sidmouth Junction–Sidmouth/Exmouth

Detached at Sidmouth Junction, two BCKs are attached to a two-car set to form a local train for Sidmouth and Exmouth. Drawn east out of the station (the junction faces London) by a BR Standard Class 3 2-6-2T this train then heads south to Ottery St Mary and Tipton St Johns, where it is divided, the two-car set and one of the BCKs bearing south-east towards Sidmouth; the other BCK is attached to another two-car set and continues via Newton Poppleford, East Budleigh, Budleigh Salterton and Littleham to Exmouth.

Below: **Standard Class 3 2-6-2T No 82019 stands with the local train at the bay platform at Sidmouth Junction as the staff await the arrival of the main-line connection in the summer of 1955.** *C. M. and J. M. Bentley collection*

Bottom: **On 9 June 1961 Standard 3 2-6-2 No 82017 leaves Tipton St John's with the 10.55am Sidmouth Junction–Sidmouth train.** *J. C. Beckett*

Above: **Sidmouth station in the summer of 1955: Standard Class 3 tank No 82019 runs out of the bay ready to back down on to its train for Sidmouth Junction.**
C. M. and J. M. Bentley collection

Right: **'M7' No 30667 near Budleigh Salterton with the 12.58pm Sidmouth Junction–Exmouth on 9 June 1961. These locomotives were much used on this line until the early 1960s, when they were replaced by the Ivatt 2-6-2 tanks.**
J. C. Beckett

From Sidmouth Junction the line sweeps downhill for nearly two miles at nearly 1 in 100 through Whimple and on to Broad Clyst. Crossing the Clyst Vale, famous for cider-making, we pass through Pinhoe before reaching Exmouth Junction, where the line from Exmouth joins from our left, before entering the tunnel at Exeter Central (formerly Queen Street), 171 miles from London.

Here our train makes its next scheduled stop, and our 'Merchant Navy' Pacific is detached and replaced by a Light Pacific — a 'West Country' or a 'Battle of Britain' — which will take us on over the 'Withered Arm' to the westerly extremities of Southern territory. Here too the two-car dining set is detached, as are the three coaches for Ilfracombe/Torrington, reducing our once-lengthy train to a mere four cars.

With our replacement locomotive at the head of the train we leave Exeter Central and run down the steep (1-in-37) incline to the Great Western station, St Davids, 172 miles from London. At this point our train, heading for the far South West, is actually facing London! This is a unique feature of this route, caused by the location of Exeter St Davids station at the foot of the incline from Exeter Central.

We leave Exeter heading north-east and pass Cowley Bridge Junction, where we part from the Great Western main line to London and cross the River Exe before reaching Newton St Cyres and Crediton. The section of line from St Davids was originally broad-gauge, the Great Western having running rights as far as Crediton.

We next reach Yeoford (183 miles from London) and a mile or so to the west pass Coleford Junction, where the line to Barnstaple diverges on our right.

Below: **The eastern approach to Exeter Central station was controlled by a large ex-LSWR signalbox, seen here on 5 July 1957 as rebuilt 'Merchant Navy' No 35023** *Holland-Afrika Line* **departs with the up 'ACE'. The carriage formation is of great interest with a mixture of Bulleid and Maunsell stock in malachite green and carmine and cream, and the locomotive, although recently rebuilt, has the earlier BR symbol on its tender. Note the large number of cattle vans in the background, and the interesting row of terraced houses on the road going down to the station.** *R. C. Riley / Transport Treasury*

Right: **Two Bulleid Pacifics stand at Exeter Central in June 1955. No 35001** *Channel Packet*, **first of the 'Merchant Navy' class, occupies the centre road; on the right, Bulleid Light Pacific No 34062** *17 Squadron* **has arrived with an up West of England train bound for London. Behind No 35001 are two Bulleid carriages in carmine-and-cream, the second of which is one of the much-despised 'tavern cars'.** *C. M. and J. M. Bentley collection*

Below right: **A general view of Exeter Central in the late 1950s, showing the centre and platform roads at the west end of the station. Note, on the far right, the train of suburban stock for local services and, centre right, the odd carriages to be added to London-bound trains. An 'M7' tank on pilot duty is just discernible at the centre of the picture, which provides a good view of the lattice-post upper-quadrant signals.** *Lens of Sutton Association*

Above: **Rebuilt 'Merchant Navy' No 35003** *Royal Mail*, **obviously well looked after, stands at Exeter Central** *c*1962, **awaiting a road for the 'ACE'.** *R. K. Blencowe*

Below: **Light Pacific No 34061** *73 Squadron* **running down the incline from Exeter Central to St Davids with the 11.30am Plymouth train on 3 July 1958. The formation is of particular interest, the uniformity of BR Mk 1s in carmine- and-cream being broken by a pair of Maunsell Open Thirds in malachite green.** *J. Scrace*

Right: Maunsell 'Z'-class 0-8-0 tank No 30951 assists a heavy train of Bulleid carriage stock up the incline from Exeter St Davids to Exeter Central on 13 June 1957. These sturdy locomotives were a common sight on this section of line at this time, having replaced the 'E1/R' 0-6-2Ts on this duty in the mid-1950s.
C. M. and J. M. Bentley collection

Below: The view west at Exeter St Davids station in the mid-1950s. Note the substantial footbridge connecting the platforms. *Lens of Sutton Association*

Top: **'T9' 4-4-0 No 30708**, in dusty black, heads Bulleid Light Pacific No 34034 as they arrive at Exeter St Davids with the up 'ACE' on 28 August 1954. The carriage stock is a mixture of Maunsell Restriction 1 vehicles, in carmine-and-cream, and Bulleid stock in malachite green. *R. C. Riley / Transport Treasury*

Above: **Bulleid Light Pacific No 34057** *Biggin Hill* leaves Exeter St Davids on 18 April 1960 with the Ilfracombe portion of the 'ACE'. To the right, on station-pilot duty, is an ex-GWR '57xx' pannier tank shunting carriages, including some Gresley bogie stock. *J. C. Beckett*

Left: On 11 April 1960 **Bulleid Light Pacific No 34069** *Hawkinge* passes Cowley Bridge Junction, Exeter, with the North Cornwall and Plymouth portions of the up 'ACE'. It was here that the WR main line to London and the Southern main line into north Devon and Cornwall parted company. *J. C. Beckett*

Right: **Bulleid Light Pacific No 34018** *Wincanton* **passes Newton St Cyres station with an Ilfracombe–Waterloo train on 1 August 1959. The locomotive is dirty and unkempt, contrasting with the sparkling paintwork of the Bulleid and Maunsell carriage stock.** *J. C. Beckett*

Left: **Maunsell 'N'-class Mogul No 31832 approaches Crediton with a Padstow–Exeter Central train on 1 August 1959. The carriage formation is made up of six Maunsell Restriction 1 carriages, four of them Brake Thirds, with a composite next to the locomotive and a Bulleid Brake Third at the rear.** *J. C. Beckett*

Below: **Yeoford station** *c*1959, **with Maunsell Mogul No 31847 running through with a local goods. This view from the platforms shows the buildings, footbridge and road overbridge.** *Lens of Sutton Association*

Coleford Junction–Ilfracombe/Torrington

Detached at Exeter Central, the Ilfracombe/Torrington portion, comprising an SK and two BCKs and hauled by another Light Pacific, branches off the main line at Coleford Junction and runs downhill all the way to the Tor estuary at Barnstaple. *En route* it passes through the wayside station at Copplestone, 186 miles from London. Here the train enters the first of the single-track sections of the line to Barnstaple, which requires token working. Soon through Morchard Road, it continues on to Lapford (190 miles), passing the milk-processing plant and approaching the first of 12 bridges that cross the River Tor, which snakes along the valley floor all the way to Barnstaple.

The railway line takes a straighter course, passing through Eggesford, Kings Nympton, Portsmouth Arms, Umberleigh and Chapelton before reaching Barnstaple Junction, 211 miles from London. Barnstaple Junction is the important hub in the local network that serves the lines to Ilfracombe, Torrington and Taunton on the former Great Western branch. Here one of the

BCKs detached from the Ilfracombe portion and coupled to another SK to form a local train for Torrington, running via Fremington, Instow, and Bideford.

Heading north from Barnstaple Junction, the two-car Ilfracombe portion crosses the iron bridge spanning the River Tor before arriving at Barnstaple Town station, a mile after the junction. Barnstaple Town was itself the junction for the narrow (2ft 0in)-gauge Lynton & Barnstaple Railway, opened in 1898 and closed by the SR in 1935.

From Barnstaple Town the train continues north through Wrafton, where a large RAF base is located, and on to Braunton, where passengers can catch a glimpse of the Crow lighthouse at Saunton Sands. From here it is faced with a climb as steep as 1 in 40 all the way up Mortehoe Bank before finally reaching Ilfracombe, 226 miles from London. The station is perched high above the town and on a clear day affords fine views across the Bristol Channel to the Welsh coast.

Above: **Bulleid Light Pacific No 34061** *73 Squadron* **at Barnstaple Junction with a train of Bulleid stock bound for Exeter Central in April 1964. The carriage formation has a Maunsell four-wheel utility van at the front and a Siphon bogie van at the rear. The town of Barnstaple is visible in the distance on the far right.** *G. Siviour*

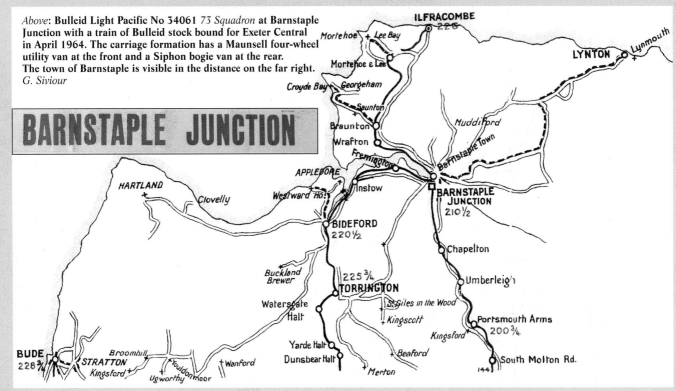

Above: Barnstaple Junction station *c*1955, viewed from the south end of the main platform. A local train waits at the platform to run south to Exeter, an 'M7' is shunting in the goods yard, and vans are awaiting unloading next to the goods shed. *R. K. Blencowe*

Below: Maunsell 'N'-class Mogul No 31847 enters Barnstaple Junction station from the Ilfracombe line with a local train in June 1960. This is where the Ilfracombe and Torrington lines part company; note the signalbox controlling this section of line. *Midland Railway Trust*

Above: **Bulleid Light Pacific No 34033** *Chard* **crosses the bridge at Barnstaple on 17 May 1964, heading for Barnstaple Town station with a local train of Bulleid and BR Mk 1 stock for Ilfracombe. The river and the town can be seen in the background.** *R. Brough / R. K. Blencowe collection*

Below: **The view south at Barnstaple Town station in the mid-1950s, with the abandoned Lynton & Barnstaple bay platform on the far left and the main buildings and level crossing in the background.** *Lens of Sutton Association*

Above: **Bulleid Light Pacific No 34080 74 Squadron** makes the climb up Mortehoe Bank with the Ilfracombe portion of the 'ACE' in April 1964. By this time, 'ACE' trains were often made up of sets of BR Mk 1 stock, as seen here. *G. Siviour*

Right: **Maunsell 'N'-class Mogul No 31406** arrives at Ilfracombe on 25 July 1964 with a through train of Stanier carriage stock from the London Midland Region. This picture shows the severity of the incline as the train enters the station, and displays to good effect the fine array of Southern Railway upper-quadrant signals at the southern end of the station. *J. H. Aston*

Right: **Bulleid Light Pacific No S21C109 Lyme Regis** stands at the platform at Ilfracombe with the 12.15pm train to Waterloo on 21 January 1949. The number carried by this locomotive, with an 'S' prefix to its original identity, represents an early attempt at renumbering the Southern fleet, abandoned following BR's introduction of a universal numbering scheme. *R. K. Blencowe*

ILFRACOMBE

Above: **A good view of the station buildings and canopy at Ilfracombe** *c*1960, **with Maunsell Moguls waiting to depart with local trains to Exeter. In the background, the carriage sidings are full of Maunsell and Bulleid carriage stock from through trains from London and elsewhere.** *Lens of Sutton Association*

Below: **Ilfracombe station, goods yard and shed** *c*1960, **with Maunsell 'N'-class Mogul No 31831 in the shed and a Bulleid Light Pacific waiting outside for attention. The extensive carriage sidings are visible in the distance, beyond the signalbox.** *SLS collection*

Above: **Fremington quay and station on 22 June 1962: Class 2MT 2-6-2T No 41216 leaves with the 2pm Barnstaple Junction–Torrington train, which is made up of ex-GWR stock.** *J. C. Beckett*

Right: **Bathed in evening sunshine, Ivatt '2MT' No 41310 simmers at the platform at Torrington, taking water after its journey from Barnstaple Junction on 25 September 1962. Note the milk tankers dotted around the yard and in front of the goods shed on the right, and the family walking up the platform, returning home after a day out. The three-car set of BR Mk 1 corridor stock behind the locomotive shows that modernity has by now reached Cornwall and north Devon.** *R. C. Riley / Transport Treasury*

Continuing our journey westwards from Coleford Junction to Padstow we pass through Bow, North Tawton and Sampford Courtenay, where we cross the East Okement River, before reaching Okehampton. This section features some very steep gradients, ranging from 1 in 100 to as steep as 1 in 77.

Okehampton, 197 miles from London, is an important market town that also serves as a hub for services to Exeter, Plymouth, Bude and Padstow. The station buildings were reconstructed in the 1930s to an art-deco design similar to that of seen at Woking and Southampton. Most of the other stations we have passed through are, by contrast, of Victorian design, dating back to the 1870s and 1880s.

The two-car Plymouth set having been detached, we depart Okehampton in what is now a two-coach train, passing to our left Meldon Quarry, which supplies stone ballast for track work to all parts of the Southern Region. The ballast leaves the quarry in trains of heavy bogie hopper wagons, hauled usually by a Maunsell Mogul. These trains travel all the way up to the yard at Woking, from where the ballast is distributed to destinations as far afield as Sussex and Kent.

We now cross the spectacular Meldon Viaduct. Built in 1874 and 183 yards in length, it crosses the West Okement River 141ft above the valley floor, on six spans of Warren truss supported by five lattice trestles. This outstanding piece of civil engineering was designed by W. R. Galbraith, Civil Engineer of the LSWR, and consists of two separate parallel viaducts which were later joined together to improve their wind resistance.

Next comes Meldon Junction, where the line to Plymouth veers away on our left.

Above right: **'U1' Mogul No 31901 was transferred to Exmouth Junction after the opening of Phase 2 of the Kent Coast electrification on 12 June 1961. In this picture it approaches Okehampton with the 3.48pm train from Exeter Central on 16 June 1961. Interestingly the train is formed of two Maunsell Brake Thirds.** *J. C. Beckett*

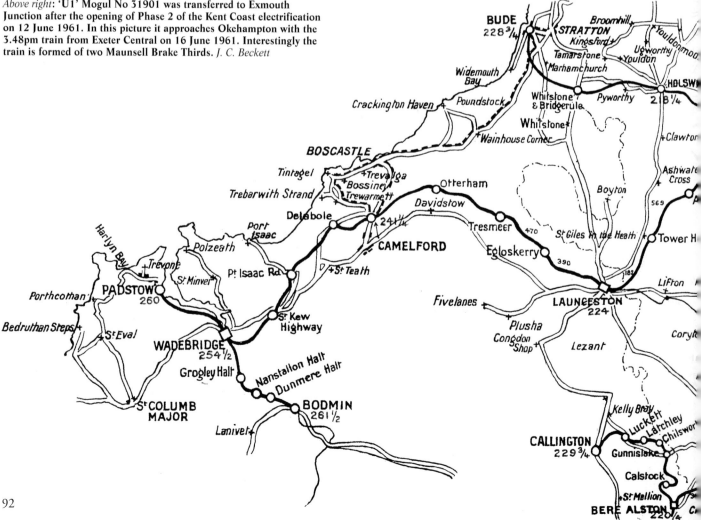

Above: Bulleid Light Pacific No 34066 *Spitfire*, which had been involved in the Lewisham accident in 1957, approaches Okehampton with the North Cornwall and Plymouth portions of the 'ACE' on 15 June 1961. The train formation is mostly made up of Maunsell bogie stock, with a restaurant car next to the locomotive. *J. C. Beckett*

Right: Okehampton locomotive shed *c*1960, with Maunsell 'N'-class Mogul No 31837 and Ivatt 2-6-2T No 41291 standing just outside the concrete shed building. The shed, which was built in the 1930s, could accommodate up to four tank locomotives or three small tender locomotives. *SLS collection*

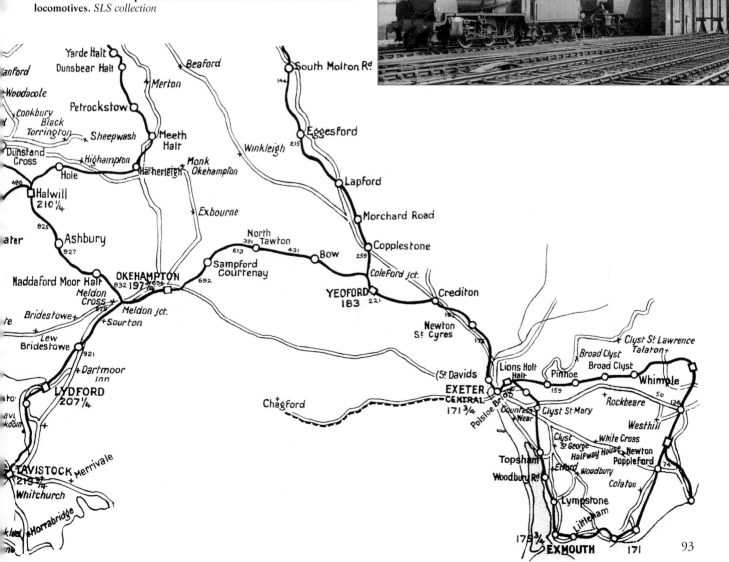

93

Above: **The view west at Okehampton station *c*1954, showing the modifications carried out in the 1930s to modernise the station from the original Victorian structure. The new canopies on both platforms have been constructed from steel and concrete. Note the footbridge and modernised buildings on the far right.**
Lens of Sutton

Below: **Okehampton on 9 September 1959, seen looking east, with Maunsell Mogul No 31841 arriving with a two-carriage local train. Note the covered footbridge and, on the far right, the goods shed.** *C. M. and J. M. Bentley collection*

Above: **Rebuilt Bulleid Light Pacific No 34034** *Honiton* **leaves Okehampton with the Plymouth portion of the 1pm Waterloo–West of England train on 16 June 1961. The stone arch beautifully frames the locomotive as the train heads west towards Meldon Viaduct and the junction for Plymouth Road.** *J. C. Beckett*

Above right: **Passing a Mogul-hauled train (including a 12-ton fitted goods van) heading in the opposite direction, 'T9' 4-4-0 No 30715 leaves Okehampton on 16 June 1961 with the 5.51pm to Padstow, consisting of four Maunsell Brake Thirds. The sidings on the left were originally used by the military. By the buffer-stops are two bogie vans used for car traffic from Surbiton, while beyond are wagonloads of new ballast from Meldon Quarry.** *J. C. Beckett*

Right: **Another view of 'T9' No 30715, sooty and unkempt but bathed in afternoon sunshine, as it heads away from Okehampton on 16 June 1961 with the 5.51pm train to Padstow.** *J. C. Beckett*

Left: **Ex-SECR Manning Wardle 0-4-0ST No 225S at Meldon Quarry *c*1925.** The quarry face itself is visible in the background, and to the right the very basic watering facilities for the locomotives. The wagons in the quarry are of interest, that on the far right, next to the quarry's steam crane, being an ex-LSWR three-plank ballast wagon; beyond the locomotive is a machinery truck, while on the far left are a collection of five- and six-plank wagons, some of them ex LBSCR, and some new SR-built five-plank opens. *Author's collection*

Right: **A later quarry shunter, 'G6' No DS3152, which served at the quarry from the early 1950s until 1962, is seen *c*1960 at Meldon, standing next to one of the ex-LSWR non-corridor bogie brake carriages used to convey quarry workers between the quarry and Okehampton station. There is a fine example of an LSWR lattice two-arm signal in the background.** *J. H. Aston*

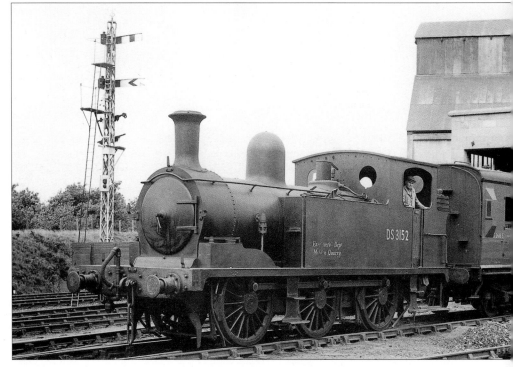

Left: **On the sunny evening of 1 August 1959 'N'-class Mogul No 31830 draws the 7.47pm Okehampton–Bude/ Padstow, on this occasion made up of four Maunsell Brake Thirds, across Meldon Viaduct. Visible in the background are the quarry and its buildings, with the distinctive locomotive shed and workers' cottages. It can be seen that the viaduct was originally two separate structures that were later joined together.** *J. C. Beckett*

Above: **An ex-GWR '43xx' 2-6-0 heads an Exeter–Plymouth train across Meldon Viaduct on 6 July 1948, illustrating an arrangement between the GWR and the Southern that allowed the two railways' locomotive crews and guards to know each other's routes from Exeter to Plymouth, against the occasions when it became necessary to work round a problem on their respective main lines.** *J. H. Aston*

Right: **In the last decade of through trains on the South Western main line a Western Region 'Warship' diesel-hydraulic, No D826 *Jupiter*, heads a Plymouth–Paddington express across Meldon Viaduct during a diversion on 26 August 1961. Note the fine rake of ex-GWR carriage stock.** *SLS collection*

Right: **In the summer of 1957 Bulleid Light Pacific No 34019 *Lundy*, having crossed Meldon Viaduct with a train for the North Cornwall line, heads west towards Meldon Junction with a formation of Maunsell and Bulleid stock. The bleak-looking quarry workings contrast sharply with the lush green fields of Devon in the background.** *C. Hogg*

Meldon Junction–Plymouth

Detached at Okehampton, the Plymouth portion, comprising a two-car set and hauled by an 'N' class Mogul heads south from Meldon Junction and begins a long and tortuous descent, mostly at a gradient of 1 in 100, which, aside from a mile-long climb from Tavistock, will continue to sea level at Bere Ferrers.

At this stage in the journey passengers have a fine view of Dartmoor on their left as the train heads south towards Bridestowe and across the River Lyd to Lydford, 207 miles from London and in Tudor times one of the most important boroughs in England. Continuing south, it runs through the station at Brentor, passing on the left Gibbet Hill, 1,035ft above sea level, where many of 'Hanging' Judge Jeffreys' victims met their end. Some 213 miles from London the train passes through Tavistock North, one of two stations in this important market town; the other is Tavistock South, the former GWR station on the Plymouth–Launceston branch, over which the train crosses on its approach.

After leaving Tavistock the train crosses the River Lumburn before heading south to Shillamill Tunnel (593yd) and proceed on to Bere Alston, junction for the Plymouth, Devonport & South Western Junction Railway, which runs from there to Callington and once served the lead and arsenic mines in this area.

Passing the junction from the PD&SWJR on the left the train runs through Bere Alston and on to Bere Ferrers before crossing the River Tavy and passing Tamerton Foliot. It is at this point that passengers have their first glimpse of Brunel's Royal Albert Bridge, a fine piece of Victorian engineering, opened in the year of his death (1859), which carries the Great Western main line over the Tamar from Devon into Cornwall.

The train is soon through St Budeaux and Victoria Road, passing Weston Mill Halt and through Ford before a encountering series of short tunnels on the approach to Devonport King's Road — the station that serves the extensive naval base, with its dry docks and repair facilities. The line is now joined on the right by the branch from Stonehouse Pool, and the train is heading east by the time it reaches Devonport Junction, where it takes to the ex-GWR main line from Cornwall. Passing the east and west junctions for Plymouth Millbay Docks, which until the outbreak of World War 2 saw considerable transatlantic traffic the train approaches its final destination of Plymouth North Road, 230 miles from London via the SR route but also the principal station for Western Region services to/from Paddington and Cornwall.

Until a year ago our train would have continued east from North Road to Lipson, there parting company with the WR main line to London and turning right through almost 180° to pass Mount Gould and Friary Junction before arriving at Plymouth Friary station, 234 miles and 5 hours from the start of its journey. This extensive terminus had been the main Southern station in Plymouth until its closure to passengers in September 1958, when it became a parcels depot and distribution point.

Below: **An unidentified Maunsell 'N'-class Mogul skirts Brentor and runs south with the Plymouth portion of the down 'ACE', consisting of two Brake Thirds, on 19 April 1963. The Great Western branch to Launceston can be seen in the foreground, while Brentor itself can be seen on the top left.** *J. C. Beckett*

Above: **Bulleid Light Pacific No 34033** *Chard* runs through Tavistock North with the down 'ACE' on 25 September 1952. The train includes two Bulleid Brake Thirds. Note the ornate station footbridge with its lattice ironwork, and the wartime paint scheme with alternating white and green supports, which had been a wartime blackout precaution. *K. G. Carr*

L. & S. W. R.
PASSENGERS
MUST CROSS LINE
BY BRIDGE

683

Left: Maunsell 'N'-class Mogul No 31836 heads the Plymouth portion of the down 'ACE' near Bere Alston on 18 April 1963. *J. C. Beckett*

Below left: **This view of Bere Alston, taken on 15 June 1961, shows the branch from Callington, which joined the main line here. The daily pick-up goods, headed by Adams 'O2' 0-4-4T No 30223, enters the station after its journey along the branch.** *J. C. Beckett*

Above: **Double-heading *c*1954: Adams 'O2' 0-4-4Ts Nos 30183 and 30216, in clean BR lined black, head a mixed train comprising a 'Gate stock' trailer and three Maunsell utility vans near Gunnislake. The leading locomotive is equipped for motor-train working, with air-brake equipment and a reservoir located on the front of the running plate.** *P. J. Bowles*

Right: **Calstock Viaduct on 21 September 1955. 'O2' No 30183 heads the 2.26pm train to Bere Alston. The locomotive is motor-fitted, and the train consists of a single utility van and a 'Gate stock' trailer.** *S. C. Nash / SLS collection*

Right: **A quiet afternoon at Callington. Ivatt Class 2MT 2-6-2T No 41315 heads a train of ex-LSWR 'Gate stock' in August 1957, shortly before this type of carriage stock was replaced by cascaded steel-bodied Maunsell stock.** *C. M. and J. M. Bentley collection*

Left: **Maunsell 'N'-class Mogul No 31856 passes through Tamerton Foliot station with the Plymouth portion of the 'ACE' on 15 June 1961.** *J. C. Beckett*

Below: **Rebuilt Bulleid Light Pacific No 34036** *Westward Ho* **heads an Exeter–Plymouth train across Tamerton Creek on 15 June 1961.** *J. C. Beckett*

Right: **Bulleid Light Pacific No 34069** *Hawkinge*, **running tender-first, crosses the Tavy bridge with the 6.48pm Tavistock–Plymouth train on 9 May 1961.** *S. C. Nash / SLS collection*

Below right: **By the late 1950s several bridges on the Southern lines in Devon and Cornwall had been upgraded to allow the slightly heavier rebuilt Bulleid Light Pacifics to run on the lines west of Exeter. Here, rebuilt Bulleid Light Pacific No 34109** *Sir Trafford Leigh-Mallory* **crosses the Tavy bridge with the 11.7am train to Plymouth on 15 June 1961.** *J. C. Beckett*

Below right: **Bulleid Light Pacific No 34069** *Hawkinge* **arrives at Plymouth North Road with a train from Exeter on 9 September 1958. The carriage stock is made up of BR Mk 1s in carmine-and-cream.** *Mike Esau*

Above: **An unidentified ex-GWR 'Hall' with a goods train crosses the junction at Devonport on 8 April 1955. This was the junction where the former GWR and LSWR lines joined for the final approach to Plymouth.** *S. V. Blencowe*

Below: **Bulleid Light Pacific No 34002** *Salisbury* **approaches Plymouth North Road with a train from Waterloo on 8 April 1955. The carriages are a mixture of green Maunsell and carmine-and-cream BR Mk 1 stock.** *S. V. Blencowe*

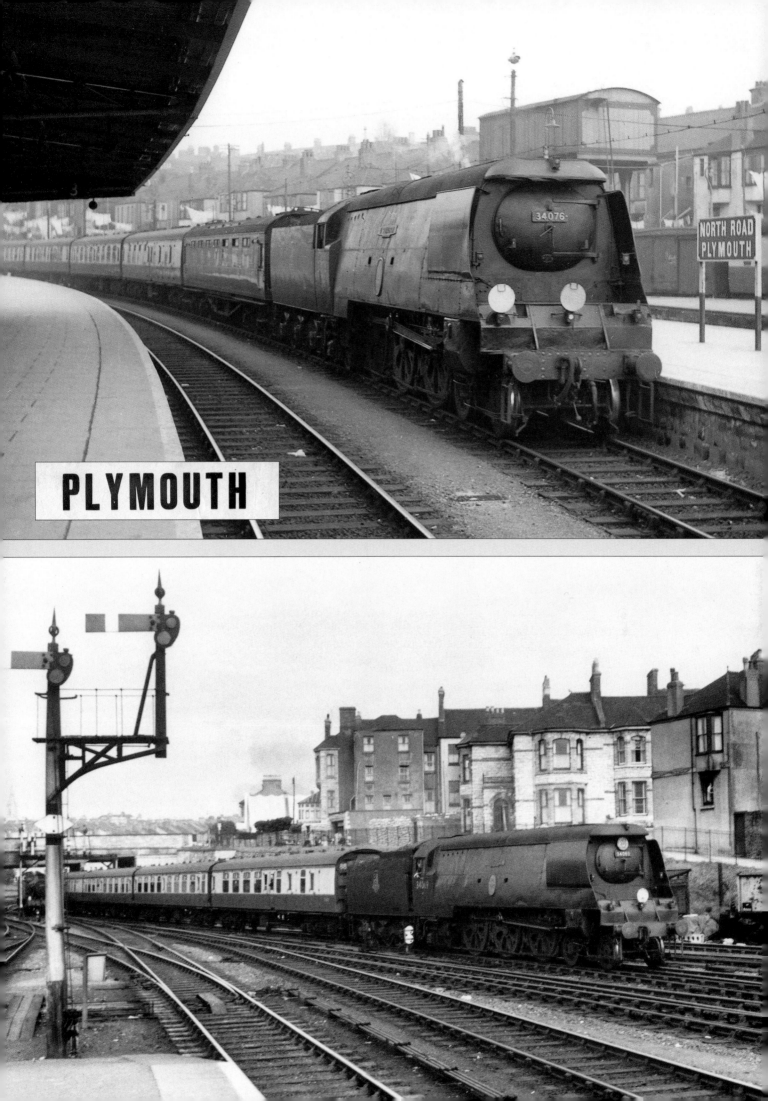

PLYMOUTH

Left: **Plymouth North Road station on 14 April 1959, with an unidentified ex-GWR 'Castle' 4-6-0 departing for Paddington. By this time the Southern services to Plymouth were terminating here, the former LSWR terminus at Friary having closed in September 1958.** *S. V. Blencowe*

Below left: **On the final leg of its journey to Plymouth Friary on 6 April 1956, Bulleid Light Pacific No 34024** *Tamar Valley* **passes Mount Gould with a train of two Bulleid carriages in carmine-and-cream.** *S. V. Blencowe*

Right: **A photograph of Plymouth Friary *c*1925, early in the Southern Railway period, showing the track layout and signalbox. Note the two 'O2' 0-4-4T locomotives on station-pilot and local-train duty, as a Drummond 'T9' 4-4-0 (centre) prepares to depart with an up express.** *Lens of Sutton Association*

Below: **Plymouth Friary in April 1957, only a year and a half before closure. 'T9' 4-4-0 No 30709 is about to leave with a three-carriage train of Bulleid stock on a local service. 'M7' 0-4-4T No 30037 is on duty as station pilot. Note the large amount of carriage stock at the platforms and in the yard, with Maunsell, Bulleid and BR Mk 1 stock all in evidence. Examples of pre-Grouping non-corridor vehicles can be seen in the background.** *S. V. Blencowe*

Resuming our journey west from Meldon Junction towards Padstow we press on through Maddaford Moor Halt and Ashbury to Halwill Junction, (210 miles from London), where the single coach for Bude is detached. This is also the junction for the North Devon & Cornwall Junction line along the Torridge valley to Torrington.

Below: **Having left Meldon Junction, 'T9' 4-4-0 No 30717 pulls away to the west and heads for Padstow with a short local train of two Maunsell bogie carriages — an Open Third and a Brake Third — on 7 July 1960. Visible on the far right, the line to Plymouth snakes away into the distance.** *J. C. Beckett*

Below left: Maunsell 'N'-class Mogul No 31840 arrives at Halwill Junction in July 1962 with a local train of mixed carriage stock consisting of BR Mk 1, Bulleid and Maunsell carriages. This station was the junction for trains to Bude, Padstow and the North Devon & Cornwall Junction Railway, which ran from here to Torrington via Marland. *E. T. Gill / R. K. Blencowe collection*

Above: On 9 August 1948 'E1/R' 0-6-2T No 2608 stands in the bay of the North Devon & Cornwall Junction line at Halwill Junction, after arriving with a train from Torrington consisting of a single ex-LSWR bogie Brake Third. The locomotive is painted in wartime plain black with Bulleid 'sunshine' lettering. The NDCJR was a separate company, with an office at Waterloo station, that had a contract with the Southern to operate its train services but had no rolling stock of its own. The line was built during the early 1920s as a job-creation project, its engineer being none other than Col Holman Fred Stephens. *Author's collection*

Centre right: Ivatt '2MT' 2-6-2s Nos 41216 and 41283 double-head a mixed train of wagons and Bulleid carriage stock crossing Marland Viaduct on its way to Halwill Junction on 24 June 1963. Visible in the foreground is one of the abandoned piers that once supported the erstwhile narrow-gauge Torrington & Marland Railway, of which some of the trackbed was used in the construction of the later standard-gauge light railway. *J. C. Beckett*

Right: Ivatt '2MT' 2-6-2T No 41312, with a single Bulleid bogie Brake Third behind, stands at Hatherleigh station on 25 September 1962 *en route* from Torrington to Halwill, while the crew chat with the local platelayer. *R. C. Riley / Transport Treasury*

Halwill Junction–Bude

Detached at Halwill Junction, the Bude portion, comprising a single BCK, is attached to a two-car set forming a local train and hauled by BR Standard Class 3. Departing westwards, this passes through Cookworthy, briefly heading due north through Dunsland Cross before bearing west to Hollacombe and on to Holsworthy, where the station has viaducts to the north and south, and continuing continue west to Whitstone & Bridgerule.

By the time the train passes through Titson and over Woolston Viaduct it has left Devon behind and crossed the border into Cornwall. It now heads briefly north-east as it passes Helebridge, finally crossing the River Neet to reach to Bude station, 228 miles from Waterloo. At one time there was a short branch which ran north for a further mile to serve a wharf at Bude harbour.

Above: **On 15 July 1957 'T9' 4-4-0 No 30717 crosses Holsworthy East Viaduct with the 1.18pm Okehampton train, comprising a four-wheel Maunsell utility van, two Maunsell Brake Thirds in carmine-and-cream and a First/Third composite in Southern malachite green.** *S. C. Nash*

Left: **In August 1957 'T9' 4-4-0 No 30708 waits at the platform at Bude while a member of staff hoses down a four-car set of Bulleid stock before the train's departure. The line of cattle vans visible in the background includes examples of GWR, LMS and LNER origin.** *C. M. and J. M. Bentley collection*

Left: **On 9 April 1956 BR Standard Class 3 2-6-2T No 82018 shunts wagons on the loop line adjacent to the station at Bude while the stock for the local train to Okehampton waits at the platform. Note the two ex-Midland-type cattle vans, far right, and the utility van in the bay platform.** *S. V. Blencowe*

Right: Standard Class 3 2-6-2T No 82010 stands at the platform at Bude with a local train for Okehampton on 9 September 1959. The platform looks very empty, with no passengers to speak of. Carriage and van stock stands in the loop and the bay platform. *C. M. and J. M. Bentley collection*

Right: Maunsell 'N'-class Mogul No 31836 prepares to leave Bude with a local train on 19 July 1963. This was the first year of Western Region management, which would prove fatal for the former Southern lines in Devon and Cornwall. Within three years this station would close, and services from here to Okehampton would be no more. *R. C. Stumpf collection*

Below: Maunsell 'N'-class Mogul No 31836 departs Bude with the up 'ACE' on 20 July 1957. Note the interesting train of mixed carriage stock at the adjacent platform, comprising a mixture of Bulleid and ex-LSWR panelled vehicles. *K. G. Carr*

We are now on the last leg of our journey, our train reduced to a single BCK, albeit still hauled by a Bulleid Light Pacific! Heading south-west from Halwill Junction we pass through Ashwater and Tower Hill and cross the River Tamar, forming Devon/Cornwall border, just east of Launceston, 224 miles from London. Here we can see on our right the GWR station, with its connecting line to Plymouth, but we continue west through Egloskerry, Tresmeer, Otterham, Camelford, Delabole (with its vast slate quarry), Port Isaac Road and St Kew Highway, then across the River Camel and thence to Wadebridge, 254 miles from London. This important junction was part of one of the first railways built in Britain, the Bodmin & Wadebridge Railway, which was one of the first lines in the South West to be taken over by the LSWR at the beginning of its westward expansion.

From Wadebridge it is but a short distance to our destination, Padstow, where we arrive at the terminus at the water's edge, 260 miles from London.

Left: **On 23 June 1959, near Launceston, Bulleid Light Pacific No 34074** *46 Squadron* **heads a two-carriage formation of Bulleid stock constituting the up 'ACE'.** *A. Linaker*

Below left: **Launceston station, July 1962: ex-GWR Small Prairie No 5544 waits to start its journey on the Great Western branch from here to Plymouth with a pair of Collett corridor bogie vehicles. Note the LSWR signalbox and, in the distance, the former GWR locomotive shed.** *E. T. Gill / R. K. Blencowe collection*

Above: **Another photograph of Launceston station, taken** *c*1960 **in the opposite direction, showing the station buildings and awning and the signalbox in the middle distance on the right. An unidentified Maunsell Mogul arrives with a pick-up goods, which it will sort and shunt into the sidings before continuing on its journey.** *Lens of Sutton Association*

Right: **Bulleid Light Pacific No 34110** *66 Squadron* **passes through Egloskerry with the Padstow portion of the up 'ACE' on 6 July 1960.** *J. C. Beckett*

Right: **On 5 July 1960 'T9' 4-4-0 No 30313 approaches Trehill Tunnel with the 3.13pm Padstow–Okehampton. The train comprises three Maunsell vehicles, an ex-LMS (Fowler) full-brake parcels van and, bringing up the rear, an ex-LMS standard 12-ton van.** *J. C. Beckett*

Left: **Bulleid Light Pacific No 34023** *Blackmore Vale* **rounds the curve into Port Isaac Road on 3 June 1960 with the 11am Waterloo–Padstow.** *J. H. Aston*

Centre Left: **A view of Wadebridge station** *c*1960, **showing the Southern Railway concrete footbridge, the LSWR-era station buildings and, far right, the locomotive shed.** *R. K. Blencowe*

Below left: **Beattie well tank No 30586 stands at the platform at Wadebridge with a mixed train for Bodmin North in June 1960. This locomotive was the one member of the surviving trio from the Bodmin–Wenford Bridge branch that was not preserved. It was arguably the most interesting of the three, in that it had the early pattern of square splashers, and of the three it was in the best condition, but it was withdrawn and cut up in 1963. This once-numerous class had been used on London suburban services until the late 1880s, when it was replaced by more-modern locomotives.** *P. H. Groom*

Right: **Ivatt '2MT' 2-6-2T No 41284 near Grogley Halt with the 2.52pm Padstow– Bodmin North, formed of Maunsell stock, on 24 April 1962.** *J. C. Beckett*

Below: **Bodmin North station** *c*1958 **with an Adams 'O2' 0-4-4T and a train of two Bulleid carriages. The station canopy and many of the station fittings seem to have been repainted recently. Note the goods platform and cattle dock in the background.** *Lens of Sutton Association*

Above: **The impressive three-span girder bridge at Little Petherick Creek, seen here on 28 May 1950 with the camera facing towards Wadebridge. This was one of the great features of this now sadly lost line, but it continues to be used by cyclists.** *J. H. Aston*

Below: **Bulleid Light Pacific No 34069** *Hawkinge* **comes off the bridge over Little Petherick Creek with the Padstow portion of the down 'ACE' on 13 June 1961. This is a fine view of the railway and the estuary it once skirted.** *J. C. Beckett*

Above: **On 13 June 1961 'T9' 4-4-0 No 30313 leaves Padstow with the 6pm train to Okehampton, comprising two Maunsell Brake Thirds and a utility van. The locomotive is one of the batch with wide splashers; the six-wheel tender indicates that it was once one of the locomotives used by the Southern in Kent and Sussex during the inter-war period. Within months all members of the 'T9' class were withdrawn, apart from the preserved example, No 120, which was restored in a spurious Adams green livery.** *J. C. Beckett*

Below: **Padstow station on 3 July 1954. In the foreground 'O2' 0-4-4T No 30200 leaves with the 4.40pm Bodmin North local train, while beyond can be seen a 'T9' 4-4-0 with narrow splashers and two sets of carriage stock from excursion trains.** *C. Saunders / R. K. Blencowe collection*

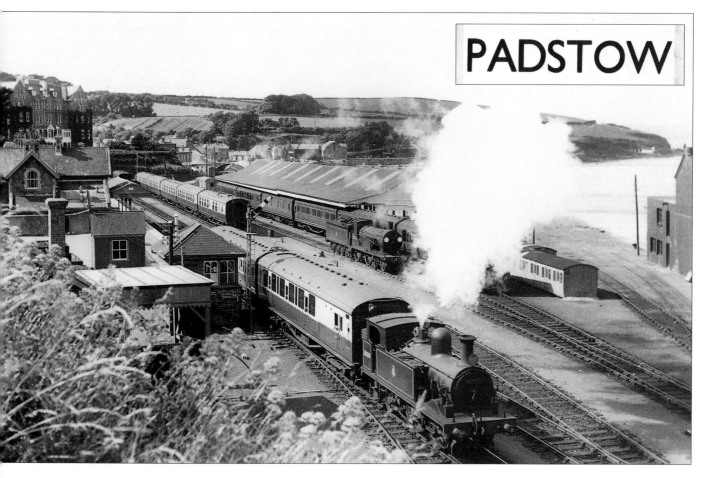

PADSTOW

Left: 'T9' 4-4-0 No 30709 simmers at the platform at Padstow with the 10.55am train for Okehampton on 1 June 1960. The photograph shows well the station building, constructed from local stone, and platform furniture. *J. H. Aston*

Below left: Padstow, 3 July 1954: Beattie well tank No 30586 stands at the platform with a two-carriage train of Maunsell stock forming the local service from Wadebridge. The summer 1954 timetable saw the Wadebridge Yard Pilot work a late morning round trip to Padstow. *C. Saunders / R. K. Blencowe collection*

Below: On 27 May 1950 Maunsell 'N'-class Mogul No 31847 waits at the platform at Padstow with the 1pm local train for Okehampton. The long building in the background, with Maunsell carriage stock standing under it, is in fact the fish sheds. *J. H. Aston*

Above: A bird's-eye view of Padstow station, showing the full track layout and infrastructure, including the station buildings, goods shed and fish sheds as they were in July 1960. The train arriving at the platform with a Bulleid Light Pacific at its head is the down 'ACE' that has just arrived from Waterloo. *Author's collection*

Below: Twilight of the 'T9s'. With the Camel estuary as a backdrop, No 30120 (nowadays preserved as part of the National Collection) is turned at Padstow on 13 June 1961. *J. C. Beckett*

The final years

Although the timings of the 'Atlantic Coast Express' improved throughout the 1950s, holiday patterns in Britain changed as more people travelled to the South West by car, until by the early 1960s this once-important train no longer enjoyed the patronage it had once boasted. Despite this, 1961 saw a final round of timetable improvements, accelerated timings from Waterloo cutting the journey time to 80 minutes to Salisbury and 160 minutes to Sidmouth Junction. Exeter was reached two minutes earlier than in previous timetables, Ilfracombe five minutes, and the connections for Torrington, Bude, Padstow and Plymouth also benefited from the accelerating timings.

The first sign of a reduction in the service came in September 1962, when the practice of detaching a through carriage at Salisbury ceased, but far worse was to come, and the Beeching report of 1963, together with the transfer, with effect from 1 January, of all former Southern lines west of Salisbury to the Western Region, sealed the fate of most of what had already become known as the 'Withered Arm'.

The Southern Region had requested a further improvement to the timings of the 'Atlantic Coast Express', which would have reduced the journey time, but it was not to be. Indeed, the management of the Western Region, determined that its route from Paddington should be the only West of England main line, wasted no time in downgrading that of its former rival. The summer of 1964 was the last for the 'Atlantic Coast Express', the service being removed from the timetable from 5 September that year at the request of the Western Region. This marked the commencement of a systematic running down not only of the former South Western main line but also of the erstwhile Southern lines in north Devon and Cornwall. Not surprisingly, most of those used by the 'Atlantic Coast Express' would close within five years of the train's demise, and the one-time Southern network west of Exeter is now but a shadow of its former self.

Below: **During the last summer of the 'ACE' the Western Region often used diesel traction over the former LSWR lines west of Exeter. On 29 August 1964 'Hymek' diesel-hydraulic No D7000 heads a train of nine Bulleid bogie carriages up Mortehoe Bank on its way to Ilfracombe, with sister locomotive No D7097 assisting at the rear.** *S. C. Nash*

Above: **An historic picture taken on 4 September 1964, the penultimate day of 'ACE' operation, showing Bulleid Light Pacific No 34015** *Exmouth* **following arrival at Padstow on the last leg of the journey from London.** *S. C. Nash*

Right: **After the end of steam on the West of England main line to Exeter in late 1964 the replacement diesel traction was supplied by the Western Region, which allocated 'Warship' diesel-hydraulic locomotives to the Waterloo–Exeter services. On 23 July 1966 No D811** *Daring* **passes Oakley station, by now closed, with an up West of England train.** *J. C. Beckett*

Right: **Okehampton in the last years of through services to/from Plymouth, Bude and Padstow. Observed from a DMU waiting at the down platform, an unidentified 'Warship' arrives with a Plymouth–Waterloo train.** *R. K. Blencowe*

Some personal recollections

Nearly half a century has elapsed since the last true 'Atlantic Coast Express' ran to points west of Exeter, but memories are long in that part of the world, and even today there are many who have fond recollections of this fast and important link with London. It therefore seems appropriate to end with two of them.

It would be convenient to record that, as I travelled frequently on the 'ACE', its fame and name are stored in indelible memories of my youth. But alas, although we walked the walk with the Southern my friends and I talked the talk more about the Great Western: we played with tiny flat-metal engine pieces on its board game 'Race to the Ocean Coast', wound up our Hornby *Caerphilly Castle* and thought the 'Cornish Riviera Express' more handsome and glamorous than its rival.

The GWR's publicity machine, with its wealth of publications and its efficient (but often distinctly authoritarian) attitude, tended to outshine that of the Southern, from which the news seemed mostly about more electrics in foggy London suburbs. The GWR's emphasis was always on its main line to the west, while over the years the Southern devoted more money to the more obviously romantic 'Belle' Pullmans than to the 'Atlantic Coast Express', which could look rather prosaic and battle-weary, especially when it had dwindled to a single coach rolling into Bude on a dull winter's afternoon. In those days our æsthetic sense was different: big, new and powerful was best (the slogan 'small is beautiful' not yet having been coined), and branch lines were poor, disregarded elements.

The Southern had the indignity of its movements westward having to pass the GWR's 'Checkpoint Charlie' at Exeter St Davids, where its trains were required to stop (although SR timetables occasionally omitted mention of this). Nevertheless, for holidays, visits to relatives and my thrice-yearly journey to school (1936-40), my family usually found itself at Waterloo a little before 11am.

The destination for holidays and family visits was generally Ilfracombe, where the station was perched attractively above the hilly, and in those days elegant, resort. For school — the remote, bible-based Christian foundation, Shebbear College — the station was Dunsland Cross, on the Bude branch, with its semi-moorland setting, usually as deserted as Edward Thomas's 'Adlestrop', but wetter. Under the station name hung a separate board for Shebbear College, and the boys who came and went formed the largest contingent ever to grace its platforms. They

were not vicious youths, but on the long-seeming journey from 'up country' they usually seized an empty compartment, pulled the blinds down against intruders and amused themselves by throwing empty Tizer bottles towards beautiful Dartmoor as they passed over Meldon Viaduct.

The complex manœuvres of the 'Atlantic Coast Express' at Exeter were enjoyable for us schoolboys, and the rich Devonian voice sonorously announcing a list of its destinations westwards, commencing with Newton St Cyres, was a regular treat; but our priority during our few minutes' shunting was a dash to the buffet to purchase a packet of Smith's crisps (then the *only* crisps), with their separate bag of salt.

Memories of the train itself are stimulated by the writings of T. W. E. Roche, who was introduced to railways at the age of seven by his doctor stepfather and whose subsequent book *The Withered Arm* (Town & Country Press, 1968) includes the following vivid recollection of Exeter Queen Street (Central): 'E449 had barely coupled up when a shriek from the cutting towards Exmouth Junction announced the approach of the train of the day, the ACE, the "Atlantic Coast Express", 11am ex Waterloo, due into Queen Street at 2.22pm, at its head almost certainly one of the "King Arthurs", 736-755 series — 744 *Maid of Astolat* or 747 *Elaine*, 751 *Etarre* or 750 *Morgan le Fay*, as likely as not.' The very names bespoke the magic of Cornwall, and King Arthur rang with Tennyson's poetry.

It seemed a shame that locomotives with such obvious West Country associations should have to come off here and make way for the nameless if elegant 'T9s', two of which would be waiting in the yard, ready to back on to the front part of the train, which consisted of the Plymouth, Padstow and Bude portions; once they had gone an 'L11', with its tall chimney, would back down on to the North Devon coaches, which included portions for Ilfracombe and Torrington to be further divided at Barnstaple Junction.

The Plymouth portion of the 'Atlantic Coast Express' was normally held for five minutes at Exeter St Davids, in accordance with the longstanding agreement with the Great Western about

Left: 'King Arthur' No 749 *Iseult* leaving Axminster station in the summer of 1928 with a down West of England express comprising a mixture of steel- and wooden-bodied carriage stock. Simmering in the bay to the left, Adams 4-4-2 radial tank No E0520 waits to depart with the branch train to Lyme Regis. This photograph shows a great deal of detail, including the 'barley-sugar twist' gas lamps, station barrows, footbridge and ex-LSWR signalbox. *C. M. and J. M. Bentley collection*

Right: **An 'M7' 0-4-4T and a Maunsell 2-6-0 head a train for Ilfracombe towards the summit of Mortehoe Bank *c*1930. The train of mixed stock has a second 'M7' tank providing banking assistance on this arduous last part of the journey from London.** *M. W. Earley*

Southern train movements through the Great Western station; this dated back to before the days when Churchward and Drummond were leading their respective companies in locomotive design. Only in summer did the crowded holiday carriages for north Devon take precedence, and, oddly, Torrington carriages were timetabled to leave Barnstaple Junction a few minutes ahead of the Ilfracombe section. Only one other train for north Devon was given the same importance, this being the overnight newspaper train, which, when I was first allowed to travel independently, gave an adventurous start to holidays as it meandered up the valley of the Tor through delicate morning mists, sparkling with the prospect of sun to come, and, it seemed, endless cloudless days of enjoyment.

My aunt's house at Ilfracombe, high up on what is still Station Road, was but a step or two from the end of the line, but the force of the west wind — often moisture-laden from the ocean and sometimes strong enough to set the observation car of the 'Devon Belle' whirling out of control on its turntable — was a huge disincentive to trudging to the harbour far below. Of course, passengers were greeted by a motley collection of road vehicles, including the green Southern National single-decker buses, off to Coombe Martin's long village street. Then there was Mr Parker's unique 20-seater, with its huge roof rack, acetylene lamps and unpainted bodywork, which, when full, and once Mr Parker had established their destinations, took passengers and their luggage to their hotels for a shilling each.

In the 1930s the resorts served by the 'Atlantic Coast Express' were largely the destinations of middle-class folk, who frequently sent their substantial luggage in advance, looked for assistance from porters on their journeys, and stayed at their chosen hotel or guest house for an average of a fortnight, making excursions by charabanc. The more important travellers would often pull rank and alight or join at stations such as Portsmouth Arms or Umberleigh, at which no stop was scheduled.

In 1947 the 'Devon Belle' Pullman train was introduced, a service that was an addition to the 'Atlantic Coast Express' as a fast train to the West Country. Unfortunately this expensive introduction ran against the current tide of travel and holiday habits. Nowhere was the change felt more rapidly than at Ilfracombe. The working classes had longer holidays, and the rapid increase in car travel, coupled with other factors, meant that instead of middle-class families dressing for dinner and afterwards strolling to listen to the brass band play as sunset faded over Hartland Point, people made brief B&B overnights, looking for brasher, noisier entertainment and grockle shops with their peppermint rock, tired fudge and kiss-me-quick hats. For the immediate future, the demand for premium rail journeys, however delightful, was over.

The writing was on the wall for most of the 'Withered Arm', and although visitors came to Ilfracombe by train in fair numbers on summer Saturdays, the mountainous gradients of 1 in 36 and 1 in 40 often required triple-heading in steam days ('M7' tanks assisting a Mogul at front and rear), making it a vastly expensive line to operate. Even with more diesel power available, the paucity of local passengers sealed its fate. When a bus could take you from Ilfracombe High Street every half-hour directly to the bus station on the riverside at Barnstaple, adjoining the town station, even enthusiastic small boys could not persuade adults to endure the alpine adventures with the train.

Douglas Stuckey

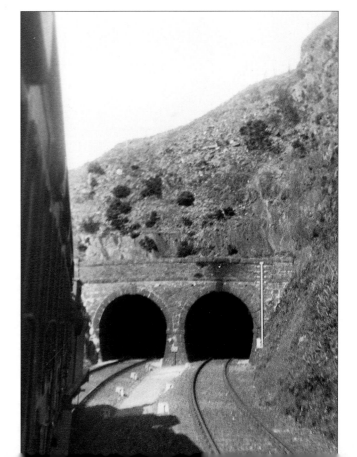

Right: **A local train from Exeter to Ilfracombe headed by an 'M7' 0-4-4T approaches the Ilfracombe tunnels in the spring of 1934.** *C. M. and J. M. Bentley collection*

It is always difficult to pull dates from the depths of childhood, but my first acquaintance with the 'Atlantic Coast Express' was in October 1947, a particularly cold day with condensation on the windows of the poorly heated carriage. My first railway memory (indeed, one of my earliest memories of anything), it is particularly valued as it recalls a journey on the Southern Railway in the last few months of its independent existence.

The 'ACE', as we often called it, was the lifeline between my home town of Plymouth and south-east London, which, perhaps unfairly, I saw as a place of exile. Always the first choice of travel, the convenience of interchange between the suburban and main-line stations at Waterloo outweighed the trek across London for the service from Paddington.

In the early 1950s I was confined to London, and the 'Atlantic Coast Express' brought visiting relations to Waterloo and took them away again. The perspective changed in the summer of 1955, when a holiday in Andover opened up the world of the train-spotter, and my first Ian Allan 'ABC' was purchased from the station bookstall. Thus were sown the seeds of a lifelong interest. The 'Atlantic Coast Express' became our timepiece, as few schoolboys had watches in those days. We would wait for the train to come through, and then walk to the other side of Andover and arrive just in time for lunch. Only once did it let us down, but, fortunately, the late running was accepted as a valid excuse. The 'Atlantic Coast Express' was sometimes diesel-hauled at this time, a progenitor of the changing face of British Railways but not yet perceived as the beginning of the end of the steam locomotive. Nor could it be imagined that in less than 10 years' time the 'Atlantic Coast Express' would be no more.

The mid-1950s brought regular returns to Plymouth; and what memories they are, in what was probably the last great swansong of the steam railway. The country was emerging from the grey years of postwar austerity; people could aspire to holidays, but most could not yet afford a motor car. The long queues across the concourse at Waterloo, the heavy leather suitcases with their straps, the occasional hatbox, porters, the long walk down the platform to find the reserved compartment in a green carriage — reservation was always wise on a summer Saturday 'Atlantic Coast Express', for not only did it guarantee a seat but it also ensured that you were in the right carriage, a sensible precaution in this multi-part train — the occasional anxiety when, minutes before departure, there was still no locomotive — then the comforting jolt as the engine backed on — and away through the south-western suburbs with their unfamiliar names.

Wimbledon and Surbiton were passed, then Woking and the countryside beyond. Farnborough was the home of the Royal Aircraft Establishment, and, although it was to be hoped that one of the pioneer aircraft of the period might be glimpsed, presumably they never flew on Saturday. Basingstoke allowed a quick glance in the direction of the engine shed, but our speed was probably in the 70s. Then Andover Junction, with its memories of where the serious interest began. The stop at Salisbury was for water and a detachment. We were now a serious distance from London, but still nowhere near our destination.

Below: **On its first working out of Waterloo, Bulleid diesel locomotive No 10203, new in shiny black, passes Vauxhall station with the 11.5am special empty stock from London to Salisbury on 6 April 1954. The three Bulleid main-line 1Co-Co1 diesels were the precursors of BR's Pilot Scheme Type 4s and spent most of their lives on the London Midland Region.** *Lens of Sutton Association*

Above: **Bulleid Light Pacific No 34106** *Lydford* **near Brentor** *c*1957 **with the 6pm Plymouth–Exeter, formed of carmine-and-cream-liveried BR Mk 1 stock.** *Mike Esau*

On my own I would never have dared alight at an intermediate station, but, when accompanied by my uncle and grandmother, it was the custom to alight at Salisbury and purchase cups of tea at the station buffet. The station was packed with people; presumably Uncle Doug knew exactly how long it took to fill a 'Merchant Navy' tender (which must surely have been longer than the five minutes allowed), but the nightmare scenario of our being marooned on Salisbury station while the train took my grandmother to Plymouth on her own haunts me to this day. The cups were of the classic British Railways pattern: thick white china with parallel sides, and handles too small to put your finger through. It amused me that, over the years, there was a steady migration of cups westward from Salisbury to Plymouth. I don't suppose anyone ever noticed that they were short of cups; but if they did, this was the reason.

The attractive countryside between Salisbury and Exeter contradicts the view held by some that southern England is overpopulated and overcrowded. The land is predominantly agricultural, with few places of major population and few sources of railway revenue. It has changed little over the intervening years; in fact it is the railway that has changed, with many of the stations gone and much of the line single-tracked. All is not necessarily well all of the time, however, and one late August Saturday in the late 1950s or very early 1960s, the train was brought to a halt for a lengthy period on what was a very hot and sunny day. The cause of the delay was never discovered, but it may have been engine failure, as a locomotive was glimpsed to the left after the train restarted. It seems to be a feature of 1950s rail travel that no one ever told you what was going on.

Although the 'Atlantic Coast Express' achieved some very creditable speeds along the Salisbury–Exeter stretch, to a young teenager, anxious to get to the land of sea, railways, fishing and Dartmoor bike rides, the journey seemed to go on for ever. Clickety-click, clickety-click, and the occasional drift of steam past a Bulleid window. Early on there have been some intriguing signs that proclaimed 'You are now entering the Strong country', illustrating the point with a picture of what appeared to be an unrebuilt 'Merchant Navy' in blue livery. This itself was interesting, as I had only ever seen a blue 'Merchant Navy' once. Many years later I was to discover that the signs advertised a brewery company. Are they still there, I wonder? Has one been preserved?

Templecombe is passed at speed — a large modern station serving a large modern town, or so it seemed, and how surprising, on visiting the shed in 1965, to find that there is virtually nothing there. Yeovil Junction flashes by some 10 minutes later, and we are now approximately halfway along the stretch between Salisbury and Exeter and approximately halfway to Plymouth. Then Chard, Axminster (but no sign of the '415' tank) and Honiton, with its inevitable stationary traffic as cars struggled to get through this notorious 1950s bottleneck. One could feel slightly superior, looking down on the struggling masses as we sped by, but the writing was on the wall, and money was spent on roads, not railways.

Sidmouth Junction, where carriages are dropped for the now-closed branches to Sidmouth, Budleigh Salterton and Exmouth, is a scheduled stop. There is much milling about at this station, which always struck me as strange, as everyone should have been sitting quietly in their proper carriages in the rear. Perhaps the crowding was such that people were standing in the corridors. There is a level crossing beyond the station, and the train has to stop before it. Again there are masses of people waiting for the gates to open, which is again str… … Sidmouth Junction is a long way f … … … tter.

Our arriv… … achievement. … … … …in is now, essential… … watershed: e… … another. Expres… status due to the ability … … … ple to a large number of holiday desti… … …ore effectively than can be achieved by any other method. The dismantling operation at Exeter Centrai … … … and there is usually much of loc… 1963, on my last journey … … … … behind the last 'Merchant Navy, … … …'lder Dempster L… was a 'W'-class tank (a type normally associa… …th the London area) stationary on one of the centre roads — a ra… …nse, as they were not at Exmouth Junction for long. Departur… …rom Central takes the train only as far as the Great Western station at St Davids, where we also stop. Great Western trains to Plymouth are, of course, facing in the opposite direction.

The Southern line departs from the Great Western main line to Paddington by crossing the River Exe at Cowley, and climbs, gently at first, through the rich and pleasant fields of Devon to Crediton, Yeoford and, climbing more steeply now, North Tawton, where the line begins to swing south-westward towards Okehampton and the northern edge of Dartmoor. The countryside is now beginning to change dramatically. Okehampton is the beginning of the end of the journey: if Plymouth is home, then Dartmoor is home territory. It is also the beginning of the arm that withered; the lines west of Meldon are now no more, and the biggest personal loss is the line to Plymouth.

The Okehampton–Plymouth route is of outstanding natural beauty. It was my custom, on leaving Okehampton, to stand in the corridor, let down the window and stick my head out all the way to Tavistock, the only warning being the rather obvious one, not to lean out too far. The crossing of Meldon Viaduct had an almost ethereal magic; suspended high above the West Okement River, gazing down on some of the wildest and most beautiful scenery in Devon, it seems not just another place but another age. Beyond the summit, just beyond Meldon Junction, the prevailing gradient is falling, although one would not think so given the ruggedness of the terrain. Yes Tor dominates, and behind it High Willhays, the highest point on Dartmoor. The wild loneliness is close but untouchable, yet you are part of it, and the railway has brought you to a beautiful place.

Good views are obtained of the locomotive, which is now a 'West Country' or 'Battle of Britain' class. Between Lydford and Tavistock the line passes close to the Great Western branch to Marsh Mills, a timely reminder that we have nearly reached our destination. Time, perhaps, to wash Pacific grime from my face, regain my seat and prepare for the final spectacle: Bere Alston, Bere Ferrers, the reserve fleet at anchor in the Tamar estuary, that lovely spot where the River Tavy flows into the Tamar, Tamerton Foliot (the station, that is, with its curious position at the end of a peninsula, a mile and a half from the place it purports to serve

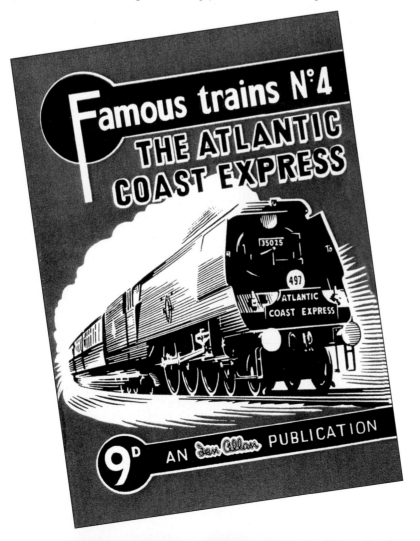

Right: 'T9' 4-4-0 No 30717 heads the Plymouth portion of the 'ACE' towards Okehampton on the first leg of its journey to Waterloo on 1 July 1960. In the background a Western Region 'Warship' diesel-hydraulic crosses the Tamar on the Royal Albert Bridge with a train bound for Paddington. Alongside, the new road bridge is under construction.
J. C. Beckett

— did anyone ever use it?), and Brunel's bridge, the view as yet unspoiled by the Tamar road bridge. Finally, the suburbs of Plymouth, Devonport King's Road and, at last, Plymouth North Road.

Once upon a time, no doubt, one could have caught a Great Western local to Laira Halt, and walked through the engine shed yard and home, but that was a long time ago. Until 1958 there was the option of staying on the train as far as Plymouth Friary, but all that did was take you on a 3¼-mile tour of the city, approaching tantalisingly close to our house at Laira as it passed behind the engine shed, only to deposit you less than ¾ mile from where you started some 10 minutes later. Better by far to take a taxi, itself a rare treat in the 1950s.

Looking back over the years of the 'Atlantic Coast Express' is a mixture of intense pleasure at having experienced them and great sorrow that one can never again make this journey. To the people of Plymouth, the line to Okehampton and Waterloo was the main line, but in the affairs of the 'Atlantic Coast Express' this was not the case. At busy periods one could be forgiven for thinking otherwise, and the motive power was usually a Light Pacific, although other classes could be used. I recall travelling midweek, to take advantage of the almost-forgotten midweek return, and surprising my grandmother, who had come to meet me at North Road. She was staring anxiously up the line, wondering what had happened to the recently announced arrival of the 'Atlantic Coast Express', not realising that the 'M7' tank and a carriage or two was, in fact, it!

The end of the 'Withered Arm' ranks with the other great closures of the period; yet the Okehampton–Plymouth seems to receive little attention. It is a pity, as it includes some magnificent scenery. The stretch from Exeter to Okehampton remains open, as does that from Plymouth to Bere Alston; it is only the line between that is actually closed. Over the years there has been talk of reopening as far as Tavistock or Okehampton, but one can appreciate the difficulties, and it is probably just talk. We shall see.

John Power

Index